Watching Things Change

Cordell J Overgaard

Table of Contents

Dedication i

Acknowledgment ii

About the Author iii

Introduction 1

The Beginning 3

Practicing Law 21

The Supreme Court 30

My Political Involvement 35

Health Care 40

My HMO Experience 42

Watching Radio Change 44

The Cable Television Experience 68

Watching Newspapers Change 75

The Steve Small Kidnapping 82

China 85

Social Media 89

Artificial Intelligence 91

Income and Wealth Inequality 93

The Broken US Political System 95

Concern About the Future 99

Dedication

To my wife, Gail, and our daughters, Susan and Diane.

Acknowledgment

I greatly appreciate the support that so many people have given to the endeavors we have shared.

About the Author

Cordell J Overgaard graduated from Harvard Law School and practiced business and corporate law for several years. He was also an owner and officer of radio stations and a cable television company, and was an officer of a newspaper company. Overgaard was active in political matters, including as a delegate to a national convention.

Introduction

I was born in 1934. Obviously, a lot has changed since then. I will write about things I was closely involved in, as well as those I was more than a little interested in.

In no particular order, I will write about my experience with the practice of law and how it changed. About my experience with radio, such as being a witness to two people unheralded today who were pioneers in the growth of FM radio, about my experience with newspapers, including my brief participation in the ownership of United Press International, and later watching the newspaper industry deal with the internet. About my experience with cable television, such as participating in the early stages of its development, about my experience with politics such as advancing for the White House during the Nixon and Ford administrations, being a delegate to a National convention and Chairman of a State Ethics Commission, I will also write about my involvement in the kidnapping and murder of a fine young man.

Unfortunately, some of the changes I will write about are extremely negative. Such is the case of two Supreme Court decisions and legislation enacted by Congress. I will also talk about what is probably the biggest change of my lifetime – Artificial Intelligence.

I am deeply concerned about the present and future of the United States.

There are some key messages for young people that I believe will come out of this paper. First, what you see today will not be the same going forward. Second, it is critical that they be able to adapt as change takes place. The second message is more important than ever because things are changing much more rapidly today. Third, people are complex, and it is important to carefully evaluate those with whom you will have a business or personal relationship. It is important to have one very clear goal - being a survivor. But always keep in mind what I call the Charlie Davis rule. Be polite and constantly say Thank You. More about this later.

The Beginning

I was born during the Great Depression. The 1920s were referred to as the roaring '20s because so much money was being made. There was substantial income inequality. Stocks rose in price. Herbert Hoover, a Republican, was elected President and took office in 1929. Upon accepting the nomination for President in 1928, Hoover said:

"We in America today are nearer to the final triumph over poverty than ever before in the history of any land. The poor house is vanishing among us."

But on October 29th, 1929, the market collapsed. There were numerous suicides. From 1929 until the late 30s, many people suffered economically. Democrat Franklin D. Roosevelt was elected president in 1932 and began a series of programs, including the creation of new agencies by executive order, referred to as the New Deal. There was considerable opposition from Republicans, but some key measures survived, including the Social Security system, Federal Deposit Insurance, and the Federal Housing Administration. Even though I was very young at the time, the depression has continuously affected my investment thinking. I have never invested totally or mostly in stocks. Instead, I always maintain cash primarily through safe debt instruments.

Fortunately, my family was a survivor during the depression, but I am not clear how they managed to accomplish that. Unemployment was very high and remained so even with the Works Progress Administration, which resulted in the federal government becoming the nation's largest employer. My father was an immigrant from Denmark, where his brothers and sisters were farmers. He was very tight-lipped, and I knew relatively little about him. I don't believe his education went beyond high school. Amazingly, he made a living as a house painter. He was self-employed and a perfectionist, which is why he was never satisfied with or retained the people he occasionally hired to work for him. He painted exteriors very infrequently but worked almost exclusively on interior work. The reason interiors were better was the walls. Interior walls back then were made of plaster and not drywall. With plaster walls, many people liked to have wallpaper. It came in many different patterns and colors. It was also more difficult to install wallpaper than to paint a wall. It was necessary to have a cutting board for wallpaper that could be cut to fit various sizes, including around doors and windows. In some situations, it was necessary to remove old wallpaper before installing new wallpaper and to fill any holes or cracks that might have appeared.

The extensive wallpaper installation process was probably such that a person like my father could charge more for it. Given that so many people were not financially well off, I have wondered how he was able to find customers. That he had a strong following was evident after his death. My mother debated whether to have a funeral home viewing before the funeral because she didn't think many people would attend, but finally decided to have the viewing. I was not able to attend. I was in the army stationed in Fort Chaffee, Arkansas, and the Red Cross failed to notify me or my superiors of the death in a timely manner. I later learned that my father's viewing was packed with many people who seemed to know each other and raved about my father. Fortunately, with the Salvation Army's help, I was able to attend the funeral.

Unless they were dressed for manual labor, workers in the 30s and 40s wore suits and ties with Stetson-type hats or formal hats with a brim. Some days, my father would leave the house wearing a suit and tie and return the same way. When he got to the customer's place, he would change into white overalls and change back when he was through working.

My mother was also Danish but had been born in the United States. She came from a very large family. Her father, who was not living, had been a Danish Lutheran pastor. She had five brothers, all of whom were well educated. Arthur was the author of a leading book on child psychology. Hans was a Danish Lutheran pastor. Adolph was a lawyer with a large Chicago bank, and Jerry was a lawyer in a successful private practice in Chicago. And then there was the mystery brother, Marvin. My mother had three sisters, one of whom was deceased. One lived in Kansas and was married to a lawyer who worked for the state government. The other was divorced from a medical goods salesman. Divorces were not as common then.

Marvin was somewhat of a mystery. He never married. A graduate of the University of Chicago Law School, he was Assistant

Vice President of the New York Central Railroad stationed in Chicago. He was an attorney of record in numerous appellate court decisions at the state and federal levels, including the United States Supreme Court. But he also had a private legal practice, where he seemed to specialize in representing wealthy widows in the Near North Side of Chicago. He was good-looking and very well dressed, and sometimes appeared in the society pages of local papers. A couple of times a year, there would be a family luncheon of the local Jersilds at the home of one of the brothers. Marvin would arrive in a limousine with a driver. It was not a rented limousine. He owned it. The driver, Sam, was his employee.

Inevitably, there would be a political discussion. All the uncles were Republicans and did not like Franklin Roosevelt. There was one contrarian. My father, who, not surprisingly, thought Roosevelt was doing well. The arguments did get somewhat heated, but my father was up against three lawyers. On the way home, my father would turn to my older brother, Mitchell, who was my parents' favorite, and say, "You're going to be a lawyer when you get older." They would frequently tell him he was going to be a lawyer. Occasionally, they would turn to me and say, "You will be too, Cordy." Parents frequently try to tell their children what they'll do when they grow up, and most of the time, they end up going in a different direction. But in my case, it became an obsession. My brother and I did become lawyers.

During the early 40s, our family lived in an apartment on the corner at 74th and Prairie on the South Side of Chicago. We lived on the second floor, and my grandmother lived in an apartment on the first floor. Pearl Harbor was attacked by the Japanese on December 7th, 1941. It was not easy to get information about the War because there was no TV and limited radio broadcasts. We were able to follow it somewhat by reading a newspaper. My mother was a secretary at the Western Union company and commuted to downtown Chicago each working day.

My brother Mitch and I attended grammar school at a Missouri Synod Lutheran Church, a few blocks from our apartment. The school had two rooms. Grades 1 through 4 were in one room, and grades 5 through 8 were in the other. About this time, I became a newspaper boy delivering the afternoon paper. At one point, I started delivering the morning newspaper, which was more difficult because most people subscribed, and I had to reload papers at various drop-off locations. There was one unforgettable tragedy. I arranged with a friend to go to downtown Chicago on a Sunday to see a movie. The Sunday paper had many inserts, so you had to deliver it from a 4-wheel cart you pushed. On the morning of the day we were to go, my friend was pushing a cart on a busy street when he was hit and killed by a drunken driver.

After finishing grammar school, my parents sent me to a Lutheran High School west of downtown Chicago. It was quite a commute to get there. It did not go well. In my sophomore year, a science teacher accused me of stealing one of his lab props. I adamantly denied doing so, but he refused to believe me. I was able to persuade my parents to let me transfer to a public high school near our home. Our home at this time was a bungalow that my father had purchased in an area in Chicago called Park Manor. It was located only a few blocks from a commuter railroad station where I and others would board a commuter train for two stops to a place close to Morgan Park High School. The teachers were excellent. It was one of the only Chicago public high schools that was racially integrated. As is the case at many high schools, there was a clique of popular students. I was not in the clique but did make several good friends.

As I was in my senior year, we had to decide what we would do next. I still could not afford to go away to a college where I would have to pay for room and board. For some reason, I became enchanted with the Coast Guard Academy in New London, Connecticut. It appealed to me because I thought I could go there, get a college education, and then go on to law school somewhere. I applied and was admitted in a process that was much simpler than getting into West Point or Annapolis. This led to my first airplane ride, something with which my friends and I were enchanted and somewhat apprehensive. When I got to the Coast Guard Academy, two things bothered me. First, cadets were required to recite obscene verses, which I found offensive. Second, and more important, I discovered that I could not enroll in law school right after finishing the four-year Academy program, but would have to serve with the Coast Guard for at least two, maybe even four years before I could attend law school. Actually, I should have known this before I went there. I soon decided that the Academy was not for me, and I resigned and went back to Chicago. Ironically, considerable publicity was given in the fall of 2023 to sexual problems the Coast Guard has long experienced.

The obvious question then was what I do now. I learned that the University of Illinois had a two-year extension program at Navy Pier in Chicago. Fortunately, I was able to enroll on time for the fall semester. I made many friends at Navy Pier. We all felt somewhat sorry for ourselves because we were missing what we thought were the fun times at the regular University of Illinois campus in Champaign, Illinois. Actually, we had it better because we had access to many nice places on the near north side of Chicago. I enrolled in business classes, and the instruction was very good.

My brother Mitch was four years older than I was, and we were not very close. That wasn't because we didn't like each other, but because we had different interests. I was interested in sports and was a big fan of the Chicago White Sox as well as the Chicago Cardinals. My parents enrolled Mitch in the University of Chicago preschool, which was a high school. He skipped his senior year of high school and went directly into college through a program administered by a person who was somewhat controversial at the time. His name was Robert Hutchins. As will become evident, Mitch played a very important role in my future.

My parents always preferred Mitch. They purchased an English bicycle for him and paid for him to bike around various places in Europe. Surprisingly, their favoritism of Mitchell did not bother me.

Mitch and I worked at various jobs whenever we could to help pay the bills. One of my jobs was as a laborer at R. R. Donnelly, which was putting together Sears catalogs. The shift started at midnight. I followed Mitch's experience and worked as a laborer for a firm that installed steel reinforcing rods to be encased in concrete for various construction projects. This was very difficult work because you had to carry heavy iron rods on your shoulder. On my first day on the job, the foreman fell off a ramp and had to be taken to the hospital. None of the workers wore helmets, and one of my supervisors had a steel plate in his head from when a wrench or something had fallen on him while he was working on a project. He also had a severe limp because of a leg injury. The hourly pay we received (over $2) was very good, which helped make the difficult job bearable.

As I was finishing my sophomore year, which was the last year I could study at the U of I Navy Pier campus, the question again became. What do I do now? I still could not afford to attend a school where I would have to pay for room and board. World War II had ended, as had the war in Korea that General Douglas MacArthur had prolonged. But talk about the military was still very prominent, as was the availability of the GI Bill. The GI Bill was intended to compensate people who had served in the military by providing funds to cover college expenses.

Even though there was no combat in 1974, the draft still existed, requiring young men to serve in the military. The most popular approach to the draft was to avoid it by obtaining a deferment or a health care exemption. I did the opposite and volunteered for the draft. My thinking was that after two years, I would have the GI Bill to pay for four years of college.

So it was that I boarded a train with other young men for a trip to the Army facility known as Camp Chaffee, which was right next to Ft Smith, Arkansas. Camp Chaffee's main function was to provide training for 105 howitzers, but it also provided 4 weeks of basic training for recruits. Basic training was not fun. Recruits were subjected to constant harassment and severe physical activity. There was also weapons training with rifles and machine guns. We even had to crawl under the wiring while machine gun bullets passed overhead. But it was not all bad. Most of the recruits had been drafted, and many had gone to college. I soon had a few good friends, which made the rigorous training process more bearable. As tough as the training sergeants and corporals were, the lieutenants were quite friendly. It was because they obtained their commissions through college ROTC programs.

We were all tested to see what we could do best. I was hoping to be sent to Germany after my four weeks of basic training and to have some sort of clerical job. But it was not to be. The test may well have indicated that I am not good at keeping track of papers, which, unfortunately, is true. I was enrolled in a four-week artillery fire direction training program rather than a four-week training program to fire a howitzer. Fire direction was one of the three prongs of artillery effectiveness. One of the prongs, of course, was the howitzer itself with a crew who would load and fire the shells. The second prong was a forward observer who would position himself in a place where he could see the desired target. The forward observer would call for test firings, which would enable fire direction to determine the observer's location and the desired target's location. Fire direction people had slide rules and other devices, but at the time, there was no computer. Fire direction training involved both classroom and field training.

At the end of my four-week fire direction training, a decision was made to have me join the administrative staff. Over time, the officers appointed me to head the enlisted men's administrative staff. The major who commanded the fire direction program put me in for an appointment from Private First Class to Corporal. However, there was a problem. The Army was not making corporals then – only Specialists. So, I wound up being a PFC in charge of a group of Specialists. This was disappointing because Specialists made more money than PFCs. But the major went ahead and called me corporal.

The 105 howitzers could be used for direct fire at an object in sight or, more commonly, targets up to five miles away. For demonstrations of direct fire, gasoline would be poured on an old tank so there would be a flash when the tank was hit. Fort Chafee was in a wooded area. One direct fire sparked a forest fire that, unfortunately, spread beyond the base into an adjacent agricultural area. The next day, there was a message posted in big letters on the message boards:

THERE WILL BE NO MORE FIRES.

By order of the Commanding General

As noted above, my father died while I was in the Army. One morning, a couple of people in the barracks told me that I had been paged the night before when they were in the base theatre. I tried to contact the Red Cross to find out what it was about, but was unsuccessful. I was able to contact the Salvation Army, which told me of my father's death and arranged for me to go to the funeral. My brother Mitch was also in the Army, stationed in Japan, and could not attend the funeral.

Before I volunteered for the draft, I was aware of USAFE, which offered correspondence courses for military personnel. I expected to use it when I was in the military. A year went by, and I had not done so. But then I took college accounting courses. I had another break. The officers in charge of the Fire Direction program were a Major and a Captain. Neither of them was a college graduate, and if they did not get their degrees within a certain time period, they would have to leave the military. So it was that on some days, I, a private first class, would get in a car with a major and a captain to drive to the College of the Ozarks, where we would take college courses. I don't remember what classes I took, but I believe one was a history class. When I subsequently applied for admission to the University of Illinois in Champaign, Illinois, I was given credit for a year of college courses because of my USAFE courses and the College of the Ozarks course.

My two-year army service would have ended at a time when it would have been too late for me to enroll in the fall semester. Consequently, I applied for early release. I said I intended to enroll in law school, and the school I was interested in, Ohio State College of Law, did not have semesters, so I would lose a year if I did not get an early release. As will be seen, I was right about the issue but wrong about the law school. I was granted early release. My official release date is September 7, 1956 – 23 months from the date I started.

In one sense, I served between two wars – the Korean War and the Vietnam War. The latter had begun earlier with various government actions that were not highly publicized. I did not really appreciate that I was in the Army Reserves after my release from active duty. I was not released from the reserves until September 30, 1962.

But my military service could have completely disappeared. For some reason, in 2006, I requested something from the government about my military service. I was shocked to get a letter from the National Personnel Records Center informing me that my records were "located in the area that suffered the most damage in the fire that occurred at this center on July 12, 1973." They sent me a copy of my DD Form 214, with the right side black and clearly scorched. Fortunately, the unburned portion of the form included most of the important information about my service, including the fact that I had been honorably discharged.

Upon my release from the Army, I enrolled in the College of Commerce at the University of Illinois in Champaign. My major was accounting. Fortunately, I was able to find housing with a friend from my Navy Pier days, Ronald Grossman. Things were going well, but I soon wished that I were more involved in campus activities. So I rushed a fraternity – Alpha Delta Phi. It was, to say the least, unusual that I, as a senior, was a pledge with the freshmen. Fortunately for me, some of the active members were veterans, and they saw to it that I was spared from some of the hazing.

Unlike today, when it is hard to get admitted into the University of Illinois, just about anyone applying at that time would be admitted because there were no other 4-year state colleges or universities. But the University did not have to keep them. Often, I would go to a local pub with some fraternity brothers for a couple of beers. When we finished, they went back to bed at the fraternity house, but I went back to my room and studied. Many of them flunked out. Although I had the GI Bill, I waited tables at a Jewish fraternity to cover my lunch and dinner.

The University of Illinois had what can only be described as a fabulous accounting department. The professors were outstanding. Some of them had their own private teaching programs focused on helping people pass the CPA exam. I signed up, and it worked. I passed the CPA exam with the second-highest grade in Illinois, for which I got a silver medal, and one of the highest grades in the United States, for which I got Honorable Mention for the Elijah Watt Sells Award.

My plan had been to attend the University of Illinois Law School. But somewhere along the way, my brother suggested that I apply to Harvard Law School. I did but with little to no thought that I would be accepted. But I was and was given a scholarship.

Harvard Law School was very different. At a session for beginning class members, we were told that the person to our right was probably the valedictorian of his graduating class, and the person on our left was probably a Rhodes Scholar. There were about 500 of us, of whom three or four were females, and one was black. The first year of law school was unique. There were no exams until the end of the year, so you would have no idea how well or poorly you were doing compared to your classmates. Harvard used the Socratic method, which meant there were no lectures. Instead, we were given reading assignments and questioned on what we thought we had learned. Most of the reading was of judicial decisions, and most of the time, the professor's questions brought out meanings I had not anticipated. The classrooms were very large and arranged with theater-style seating, with the back seats higher than the front. The rear seats were in high demand because we did not want to be called on by the professor. There was at least one exception where a person would raise his hand when the professor called for someone to answer a question. Virtually every time, the student's answer was incorrect. The student was Michael Dukakis, who went on to serve two terms as governor of Massachusetts. He ran for President in 1988 against George H. W. Bush and is known for something he did during his campaign that turned off many voters. He was filmed driving an M1 Abrams tank while wearing a helmet.

There were social differences at the law school. When I first got there, I could carry on a good conversation with a fellow student until he asked me where I graduated from college. Unless I said an Ivy

League school, he would say "Oh" and turn away. There were two clubs for law students. The Lincoln Inn Society was for graduates of Ivy League schools, and the Chancery Club was for graduates of other schools. But as the school year progressed with the Socratic teaching method, everyone became humbled, and the previous differences dissipated.

I studied constantly during my first year, and it may have been a mistake. When we got to the end of the year, there was a week or so for people to study for exams. But I couldn't study. Try as I might, I could not study, and I became very depressed. So depressed that I flew back home to Chicago and was prepared to give it all up. But my mother wouldn't have it. You must go back and give it your best. So I did. I took all the exams and wasn't sure how I did.

It turned out that I did not do badly. I finished in the top 50 out of a class of about 500 and was awarded a spot on the Legal Aid Society. The people with the best grades were named to the Law Review. The next six or so were named to the Board of Student Advisors, and the rest of the 50 were named to the Legal Aid Society.

I spent the summer between my first and second years clerking at a CPA firm – Price Waterhouse. Half the summer was spent with the auditors and the other half with the tax department. I was sent to Casper, Wyoming, to participate in the audit of a large oil firm. Company audits were performed with an audit program that spelled out what the auditors were to look at. The program indicated that I was to review a report that was prepared by the company's staff. But the staff told me that they did not prepare such a report. My accounting training suggested to me that in such a situation, I needed to dig further to find the facts that the report would have produced. I then proceeded with such an investigation. It came back to haunt me. When I was interviewed at the end of the summer, the company person praised my work, but then said, "But there is one thing. When you were working on the audit in Casper, you spent a substantial amount of time digging into various files. There is a limit to how much time we can spend on matters because we are in business to make money."

When I returned to Harvard for my second year, I was still depressed. I went to the Harvard health department for help dealing with my situation and talked to a psychologist. When I had finished explaining my situation and answering his questions, I asked him when I would see him again. You are strong, he said, and can handle this by yourself. You don't need to see me. He was right. I was able to recover by myself.

I remember the second year at Harvard Law School as just being one of many classes and a lot of studying. But there was no fear experienced during the first year. The summer between the second and third years was very memorable. Memorable because I met and married Gail. Gail lived in McKeesport, Pennsylvania, but came to Chicago to visit a sorority sister. On a Sunday, a group of us went to the Lake Michigan sand dunes on the Michigan side for an afternoon of fun. Things moved rapidly. Gail and I dated, and the next thing we knew, I was in McKeesport to marry her. An elaborate wedding it was not. But a great one it was.

I worked that summer with a law firm in Chicago that represented a large local public utility. It had a small tax practice with a great tax lawyer. My work was cut short when I got word that I had been elected to the Harvard Law Review and needed to come back to the law school early. I made the Law Review because I finished 6th in my second year. So Gail and I packed and drove to Cambridge, where we rented an apartment. To help pay the costs, Gail got a job in the beauty department of a drug store in Harvard Square.

There was a saying that in the first year, Harvard Law School scared you to death. In the second year, it worked you to death, and in the third year, it bored you to death. I found this to be accurate. Being on the Law Review meant that you would work at the Gannett House, an old building, and associate with people considered very smart. At that time, membership was determined solely by grades. It is now determined by a writing contest. Harvard Law School published seven booklets each year that featured law articles by prominent legal professionals as well as relatively short anonymous articles written by Review members. I wrote an article that made little sense to me then.

Harvard Law Review has produced several lawyers who went on to important government or judicial positions. Among them is Barack Obama. One of my classmates, Antonin Scalia, went on to become a Supreme Court Justice. We called him Nino. As noted, he wrote the majority opinion in several key decisions.

The third year of Law School is when you look for a position after you graduate. As a member of the Law Review, I was in a good position. I made some career-defining decisions. I could have been hired by a major New York law firm where there was plenty of money to be made. But I decided not to pursue that alternative. For whatever reason, I was determined to go back to Chicago. I did an interview at Jones Day, a major law firm in Cleveland, but I decided against working there. I was still focused on being a tax lawyer, and one of the top tax firms in Chicago was Hopkins Sutter. The firm invited Gail and me to a friendly evening at the home of one of its partners, Dan Walker. Dan was not a tax lawyer, but he and his wife, Roberta, were very warm and friendly.

Practicing Law

I did not interview at other Chicago firms and accepted a position with Hopkins & Sutter. I chose the firm because it was one of the two top firms in Chicago for federal income tax matters, and I thought this fit with the fact that I had passed the CPA exam. The firm did have a broad practice, and I was told I would not be limited to working on tax matters. The three top senior partners had their own fiefdoms. Andy Owen was a brilliant lawyer who represented public and private corporations as well as wealthy individuals. He was very hard on associates and had a bad memory for names. He called me "Babe" for several months. He worked long hours and, unfortunately, would often have me sit in his office while he was drafting documents. However, he did take time for us to go to a restaurant in the building for dinner, during which he enjoyed a martini. I would rather have gone on working so I could go home earlier.

Tom Mulroy was a litigator, although he rarely participated in a trial. His forte was representing businesses and individuals that were defendants in business lawsuits, frequently derivative actions. Mulroy was a charmer. He was so good at charming people that when he severely criticized an associate, the associate felt good.

Charlie Davis only handled federal income tax matters and was very good at it. He also had good ties to the staff of the House Ways and

Means Committee. Davis had two unusual characteristics. He sat silent most of the time during meetings while the other participants frequently said stupid things. His silence was interpreted as brilliance. The second characteristic was politeness. When you were walking somewhere, he would step to the side and make sure other people could go ahead of him. He was constantly thanking people, which is the basis for my Charlie Davis Thank You rule.

My only experience as a trial lawyer came when I assisted Davis in a tax trial in the federal district court in Chicago. As is frequently the case, the facts and law were very complicated. The judge seemed to be dozing at various times during the trial. At one point, I had a problem with what the government's attorney was saying, and I stood up and loudly said, "Objection!" The judge came to life, turned toward me, and said in a stern voice, "Sit down, young man."

Hopkins & Sutter had only about 28 lawyers when I joined. Very few law firms at that time had more than 100 lawyers. I started at $6,700 a year, though I received a small Christmas bonus. Some firms were paying $7,200 annually. Hopkins & Sutter had two offices - the main office in Chicago and a small one-person office in Washington, D.C. that primarily performed various functions for Charlie Davis and his tax practice. It was very unusual then for a law firm to have more than one office.

I spent most of my time on business matters – primarily acquisitions, including mergers. Initially, this was for Andy Owen's client – Consolidated Foods Corporation. Consolidated was a conglomerate with various food-industry subsidiaries. Probably its best-known subsidiary was Sara Lee, which was known for its pastries, particularly cheesecake. The acquisitions took me to various parts of the country, where I worked with lawyers for the other party to the transaction. Certain provisions were common to most acquisition agreements, and negotiations typically focused on how they would apply in a particular transaction. The lawyers I dealt with were experienced, and the negotiations, although sometimes lengthy, were conducted in a polite, business-like manner. On more than one occasion, the opposing lawyer would later send me legal business.

Consolidated's Chief Executive Officer and principal shareholder was Nathan Cummings, who had a large collection of expensive paintings. His two sons became clients of mine personally, although one of them, Alan Cummings, died at an early age. At one point, Consolidated offered me the position of General Counsel. After discussing the offer with Andy Owen, I declined the offer. Of course, it then hired someone else, and predictably, our Consolidated legal business declined.

I also did substantial legal work for another client of Andy Owen, Cahners Publishing Company. Initially, Cahners' primary business was publishing trade magazines, but it expanded into other areas over time. Cahners had an office in Chicago, but its main office was in Boston, and I made many business trips to the city. Cahners was owned 40% by Reed International, a British company, and one of our meetings was in London. When Andy Owen retired, the Cahners people asked him who would succeed him as the principal outside attorney. "Ken Pursley," Andy said, because he seemed to have become a little concerned about my independence. "Thank you," Norman Cahners said, "but we prefer Cordy Overgaard."

As time went on, Reed purchased the remaining 60 per cent and became the sole owner of Cahners. During the acquisition negotiations, Norman Cahners asked the British for a commitment that I would continue to serve as Cahners' chief outside counsel. The British agreed, but as soon as the deal closed, they replaced me with the lawyer who had represented them in the negotiations. I learned from the Cahners people that the lawyer had lied to the British about the difficulties I created during the acquisition negotiations. Ironically, the lawyer's firm collapsed a year or two later.

At one point, I served as the firm's counsel to Chicago Bridge & Iron Company, a publicly held corporation based in Oak Brook, Illinois, until it was acquired by another corporation.

One day, one of my partners asked me to meet a young man who was in his second or third year at Harvard Law School and was summer clerking with some Chicago firms. His name was Barack Obama. It was a very brief conversation.

My legal work on acquisitions took me to various parts of the country, where I worked with lawyers for the other party to the transaction. Certain provisions were common to most acquisition agreements, and negotiations typically focused on how they would apply in a particular transaction. The lawyer I dealt with was experienced, and the negotiations, although sometimes lengthy, were conducted in a polite, businesslike manner. On more than one occasion, the opposing lawyer would later send me legal business.

When I started my legal career, the law was considered a profession, and lawyers in firms like mine were generally respected by laypeople. Of course, lawyers are expected to make a decent living, but making a lot of money was not an obsession. This changed, and there were various reasons for this.

Some opposing lawyers began taking arbitrary, clearly unacceptable positions, and it was obvious they were working to generate higher fees. Firms became more business-oriented and began opening offices in other cities. A forerunner of what was to come was the law firm Finley Kumble. Started in 1968 by two lawyers in New York, it began hiring successful lawyers from other firms by offering what were then staggering sums. It also recruited retired politicians, including Robert F Wagner, the former mayor of New York City. Finley Kumble aggressively promoted itself and grew to nearly 700 lawyers, with offices in several cities across the United States and in London. The amount of fees brought in was overwhelmingly the criterion for partner compensation. But its demise came in 1987 because of nasty infighting among its partners and the fact that its partner distributions were largely financed by borrowings rather than fee revenue. The machinations at Finley Kumble were described in great detail by Kim Isaac Eisler in his book *Shark Tank, Greed, Politics and the Collapse of Finley Kumble, One of the Largest Law Firms.*

A major development occurred in 1978 when Steven Brill started a magazine called *American Lawyer. T*he magazine reported on what was going on with lawyers in the larger firms, including some matters that were not very flattering. In short order, the magazine began publishing the amounts partners were making at large law firms. Not surprisingly, it got the attention of lawyers who saw that some of their peers were making more. In some cases, substantially more. It soon led to some lawyers jumping ship and becoming lateral hires at other firms. It also created pressure on law firm managers to increase profitability so partners could make more.

Firms began increasing their fees as great emphasis was placed on billable hours, both as a criterion for billing and also for associate and some partners' accountability. Young lawyers were expected to have 2,000 or more billable hours annually. I'll never forget the time I was standing at a urinal in the men's room at the firm and mentioned to an associate who was at the adjoining urinal that I might want to use him on a matter I was working on. I did not, in fact, use him, but when I later got the *pro forma,* a listing of billable hours for the matter by attorneys, I discovered he had recorded 1/4 hour for a conference with CJO. There were many times when I would get ready to bill one of my clients, and I would be troubled by the number of hours some lawyers spent on matters. I knew what was involved and that it shouldn't take that much time. Invariably, in those situations, I cut the number of hours

I billed. It was about this time that I changed hats. I gave up the lawyer hat for a client hat.

Hopkins & Sutter had a partner retirement program that was very generous -too generous for retired partners. It was wisely decided to change the program. I was delegating a substantial portion of my acquisition work to young lawyers whom I had trained. So, I decided to retire and take advantage of the retirement program while it was still in effect. But neither my partners nor I wanted me to disassociate completely. So, we entered into a retirement agreement where I changed from an equity partner to an income partner with guaranteed annual, decreasing payments over three years. I was virtually free to spend as much or as little time practicing law as I desired, but I continued to bring in new business.

After I was fully retired, I shifted the legal work for a newspaper company I was involved with, as well as my radio station business, from Hopkins & Sutter to a firm in Cedar Rapids, Iowa, that provided quality work at considerably lower fees. One of the partners had been an excellent associate with my old firm, and I was very familiar with him.

Not surprisingly, the increased emphasis at law firms on billable hours created some problems, as noted by Stephen J Harper in his book *The Lawyer Bubble*:

"Besides putting the attorney's self-interest in billing more time against the interest of the client who pays the bills, the regime also encourages lawyers to 'pad' their time. That lawyers speak of fraud.

Because attorneys self-report their client hours, time billed but not actually worked usually goes undetected. Walter Hubbell, a former chair of the Arkansas Bar ethics Committee and state Supreme Court Justice before becoming a high-ranking official in the US Department of Justice during the Clinton administration, was a partner in a prestigious law firm when he billed clients for time he never worked. Eventually, he went to prison for it. Another partner at a prominent Chicago firm got into trouble when someone questioned how he could bill almost 6,000 hours annually over four consecutive years. The answer was he couldn't." ((pp79-80)

Another development was the rise of multi-city law firms. Part of this trend was accomplished by law firm mergers, which became quite common. My old Firm, Hopkins & Sutter, merged with Foley & Lardner, a Milwaukee firm. As firms got bigger, traditional law firm practices changed.

In many firms, equity partners rose in lockstep, meaning their share of partnership profits increased with longevity, so partners who were effective lawyers but not business-getters were rewarded. No more equity shares depended on billings.

In many firms, an equity partner would not be de-equitized unless they committed some egregious act—no more. Firms ousted partners, sometimes in mass, when they wanted to cut expenses.

The ratio of associates to partners changed dramatically at many firms as they sought to improve profitability by increasing the number of associates to create greater leverage.

Over the years, more changes have occurred. The largest law firms now have over a thousand lawyers, and some partners earn several million dollars a year. In a 2024 article in Harvard Law Today, Professor David Wilkins noted that a majority of law firm associates are now women.

Artificial intelligence is expected to make major changes in some practice areas in the years ahead. It could potentially reduce the time spent on many matters and the number of associates needed. It will be interesting to see the extent to which outside provider firms will use AI to take more business away from law firms and how law firms will adjust to this development. It has the potential to affect law firm profitability significantly.

The Supreme Court

As noted above, there were very few lectures in my first year of law school because Harvard used the Socratic Method. The professor would assign case opinions for us to read, and the next day, there would be questions about them. We did learn about key Supreme Court justices of the past. John Marshall was one of the most significant. He presided over the Court when it first ruled that it had the power to declare federal legislation unconstitutional. Other key justices were Louis Brandeis and Oliver Wendell Holmes. One of my favorites was Justice Jackson because his opinions got to the point.

The decision process is very complex. Very few cases appealed to the Supreme Court are considered by the court. Those that are typically have several briefs presented to the court by both sides of a case. Time has not made the process easier, because the court has to consider how the issues in the case before it have been dealt with in earlier cases, of which there are now many. This is because of *stare decisis,* meaning, in Latin, to stand by things decided, which is a legal principle that directs the court to adhere to previous judgments. But the Supreme Court can and sometimes does decide that stare decisis is no longer valid.

In cases involving interpreting the Constitution, there are three commonly used methods of interpretation: textualism, originalism, and pragmatism. Textualism focuses on the plain meaning of the text of a legal document.

Originalism focuses on the public meaning of the Constitution and its amendments at the time of their adoption. Pragmatism focuses on the words of the Constitution and the practical consequences of the interpretation.

These definitions are easier to write than to practice. In the case of originalism, things were quite different when the Constitution was enacted. For example, women did not have the same rights then as they later did. Two Justices of the past held personal interpretations. Justice Holmes believed that justices should not make new laws based on their personal beliefs. (judicial restraint). Justice Brandeis believed the Constitution to be a "living document" that had to be interpreted in light of changing times. (judicial activism).

The Second Amendment provides an interesting case for interpreting the Constitution. It provides:

"A well-regulated militia being necessary to the security of a free state, the right of the people to bear and keep arms shall not be infringed."

The key question is whether the italicized language, sometimes referred to as the preparatory language, and the remaining language, sometimes called the operative language, are to be considered together or whether the operative language stands by itself. In 1939, the Supreme Court adopted what is called a collective rights approach, but in 2008, in a five-to-four decision, the Court adopted the individual rights approach, which dismisses the preparatory language.

The majority opinion was written by Justice Anton Scalia. Dissenting opinions were written by Justices Stevens and Breyer. Scalia viewed his decision as a major example of the Originalism approach.

According to an article in the Atlantic, 15 eminent university professors submitted an amicus brief that said in part, "But as historians of the Revolutionary era we are confident at least of this: that the authors of the Second Amendment would be flabbergasted to learn that In endorsing the republican principle of a well-regulated militia, they were also precluding restrictions on such potentially dangerous property as firearms which government had always regulated when there was 'real danger of public injury from individuals'"

After reviewing the majority and dissenting opinions, I strongly believe the case was wrongly decided. Moreover, it opened the door to astronomical gun violence and many thousands of deaths.

Another Supreme Court case that was wrongly decided is Citizens United, which enables massive political contributions and is discussed in some detail below.

I believe that an additional constitution interpretation method must be added -Political. And that is the method now used most by the majority of Supreme Court members.

Questions have been raised about the lack of a Supreme Court code of ethics. Justice Clarence Thomas has received numerous free trips and other benefits. According to the book *The Justice of Contradictions,* "From 2004 until the time of his death, [Scalia] had taken more than 250 privately funded trips." Calls for an ethics code have been resisted by the Chief Justice. It isn't easy to imagine that free trips have not influenced any of the justices' decisions.

A further problem with our judicial system is delay. It takes too long for cases to get through the courts. Some cases are more important than others from a timing standpoint. An example of this problem has to do with the tariffs imposed by President Trump. A special court held that some of them were illegal, and the Circuit Court affirmed the decision on appeal. The decision has been appealed to the Supreme Court, but its decision will not be available for some time. It is incredible because if the decision is affirmed, the federal government will have to return millions of dollars it has collected with tariffs, and the decision will have a huge international impact.

By the time most cases reach the Supreme Court, arguments for and against the issues at hand will have been presented by counsel for the various sides. Similarly, the arguments will have been reviewed by judicial clerks. So, the judges are not starting from scratch when they consider a case.

I am concerned about the tendency, in cases involving statutory interpretation, to avoid reliance on specific language and to interpret other language as producing a result. An example is the case about the legality of Trump's tariffs. The statute in question (IEEPA) authorizes the President to take certain action in response to an unusual and extraordinary threat. In holding that the statute does not authorize tariffs, the Circuit of Appeals said that none of the actions mentioned in the statute "explicitly include the power to impose tariffs, duties or the like, or the power to tax."

But the government argued that "the term 'regulate …importation'" gave such authority, an argument rejected by the court.

My Political Involvement

Gail and I had originally settled in a southern suburb of Chicago primarily because my brother Mitch lived in the southern suburb of Homewood, where he practiced law in addition to an office in downtown Chicago. But we soon moved to Evanston, where one of my law school classmates lived with his wife. We purchased a two-story home for $26,500.

While in law school, I kept up with current affairs but was not active with any political party. That changed in Evanston when I became very active in the Evanston Young Republican Organization, which had an active membership. I also became active in state and local elections, supporting the Republican candidate. The Republican Party was totally different then. There were several good Republican officeholders, such as Senator Chuck Percy and the Cook County Sheriff, Richard Ogilvie.

At one point, I was the subject of an article in the Chicago Daily News with the headline, **Young GOP Warned of Bircher Threat.** It began by saying, "Cordell J. Overgaard, President of the Evanston Young Republicans, said Friday that John Birchers are attempting to take control of his organization." Suffice it to say, they did not succeed.

Daniel Walker left Hopkins & Sutter and became Montgomery Ward's General Counsel. Ironically, I briefly represented Montgomery Ward management some years later. Walker ran for Illinois Governor and was elected partly because he "walked the State." After his election, he formed a Board of Ethics to oversee the ethics of state government-appointed officials. The Board had three members: two Democrats and one Republican. He appointed me the Republican member. Walker served from 1973 to 1977 but was defeated for re-election by James Thompson. Walker's Board required key government workers to submit a copy of their personal income tax return to the Board.

I wrote a critique of the Board after the election and said that income tax filing should not be required. Shortly after Thompson was elected, I attended a meeting of the Chicago Bar Association Corporation Committee where Thompson was the main speaker. Thompson said he was appointing Cordell Overgaard as the new Chairman of the Board. I was astonished but obviously accepted. I changed the Board's approach to be similar to that of a government agency, where you can submit information about the action you propose and request a "no action" letter. Walker went on to get involved in various matters and ultimately was convicted of federal crimes involving a savings and loan association with which he was involved.

One of the Republicans I got to know was Donald Rumsfeld, then our local Congressman. Rumsfeld got to know me because I was in the local news for being opposed to the John Birch Society. Rumsfeld became active in the Nixon administration, and when Nixon ran for re-election in 1972, Rumsfeld submitted my name as a possible part-time Presidential Advance Man. I accepted. I attended a meeting of advance men in the White House shortly after Watergate. One of the people in attendance was Jeb Magruder, who was then a staff member. I had known Magruder from my Young Republican days, and I am sure he knew me, but he acted at the meeting as though I were a stranger.

I advanced two events of Nixon's daughters and one event involving Nixon. That event was a drive-through where Nixon was driving across Ohio. I was assigned to build a huge crowd in Columbus for when he drove through. As was customary, I arrived in the Columbus area a few days early. I visited the local county politicians to get help with crowd building. They were worthless. Somehow, I got to know a local teacher who had many friends. With his help, we lined up three high school bands to serenade the president. The crowd was huge, but when the appointed time came for the President to appear, he was nowhere to be seen. Time kept passing, and I was worried that people would disperse. To hopefully prevent that, we started marching our bands back and forth on the main street. And then the buzzing began as the motorcade came in sight. When the president's limousine came to the main intersection, the car stopped. A glass partition on the roof of the limousine slid away, and Nixon stood up, microphone in hand, and gave a short speech. The chief advance man found me and was ecstatic about the crowd.

Watergate was a terrible national experience. So why did I support Nixon for President? Because of his record before then. He had several domestic accomplishments, including the creation of the Environmental Protection Agency, increasing Social Security payments, and increasing the number of women in policy-making roles.

He also reopened diplomatic relations with China. His popularity was such that he won 49 states for re-election in 1972. I was not then aware of the bad things he talked about in secret with Haldeman and others.

Gail and I attended Nixon's second-term inauguration and some of the events. I later served as an advance man for President Ford and was a Republican delegate at the Convention where he was nominated for a full term.

I continued to be a Republican and voted for Republican Presidential candidates. But one thing changed my political allegiance—the decision by George W. Bush to invade Iraq. I was stunned to watch on TV as bombs were exploding in Iraq. Why are we doing this, I said to myself. My Republican friends disagreed with me but subsequently agreed.

While I lived in Illinois, I had the feeling that members of the Republican and Democratic House and Senate had disagreements but got along fairly well. There were even reports that some opposing party senators would get together for a drink at the end of the day. There were some anomalies. One was Joseph McCarthy, who was a Republican senator from Wisconsin. In 1950, he made news by claiming he had a list of Communist Party members employed in the State Department. He subsequently made other similar charges, which gained him considerable publicity. Later, he was confronted at a Senate hearing by attorney Joseph Welch, who at one point said, "Have you no decency?" McCarthy was usually accompanied by Roy Cohn, who subsequently became an adviser to Donald Trump. The Senate ultimately censured McCarthy by a vote of 67 to 22.

Things changed. Bipartisanship disappeared from the House and Senate. The two Republicans who have received the most criticism for obstructing bipartisanship are Newt Gingrich and Mitch McConnell.

I have tended to vote for Democrats. I was very pleased with Obama. Although I voted for Biden, I was not enthusiastic about his Presidency. He promoted legislation that is commendable for its potential to advance important business projects in future years, but he basically ignored the concerns many people had about living costs and the economy. He also mishandled the Afghanistan withdrawal and made a major mistake in appointing Merrick Garland as Attorney General. Garland probably would have been a great Supreme Court Justice, the position to which he was initially nominated, but he was not the kind of person to be Attorney General.

Health Care

Health Care in the United States is poor compared to other countries. A 2024 Mirror Mirror report of the Commonwealth Fund compared health system performance in 10 countries, including the United States. It concluded that "The U.S. continues to be in a class by itself in the underperformance of its health care sector." It also found that "[i]t's an outlier on health care spending as well."

Among the reasons given for higher medical costs in the U.S. are the following:

1. Drug costs. Americans pay almost twice as much for prescription drugs as people in other industrialized countries. A major reason for this is that drug prices are not government-regulated.

2. American doctors have higher incomes than doctors in other countries. This may be because the U.S. is underserved. According to the Health System Tracker, the United States has only 0.6 general practitioners per 1,000 population compared to a comparable country average of 1.4.

3. Varying healthcare prices. The healthcare system is complex and varies depending on location and provider. Some hospitals

have been acquired by private equity firms, which are profit-oriented.

4. Complexity. Health care is provided by a multitude of different providers with different pricing policies.

Unlike most countries, the United States does not have universal healthcare. A combination of government programs, private insurance, and employer-sponsored insurance covers healthcare expenses. Many people in the United States do not have any medical cost coverage.

According to The Commonwealth Fund Mirror, Mirror report:

- The U.S. spent more than 16 percent of its gross domestic product on health care in 2022. Other countries spent between 8 and 12 percent.

- U.S. life expectancy is more than 4 years below the 10-country average.

- The U.S. ranks 9th in administrative efficiency.

The US health care system will likely become a bigger problem in the years ahead. At the very least, the government in the US should regulate drug prices. Unfortunately, this is unlikely to happen due to political opposition.

My HMO Experience

At one point, I became more than a patient.

Gail and I had a doctor in Evanston whom we liked very much. His name was Arnie Wyden. One day, he told us he could no longer have us as patients unless we joined a health management organization ("HMO") he was about to lead. Its name was NorthCare, and it was formed with good intentions but totally unrealistic policies. It provided health care to just about everybody in the community who asked for it without regard to whether they could pay any part of the cost.

At Wyden's request, I became a member and subsequently President of the Board of Directors. It soon became evident that NorthCare could not survive financially very long. Fortunately, we were approached by a health care corporation that was interested in acquiring Northcare. It was not easy to conceal our eagerness for a deal during the negotiations.

Because NorthCare was a membership organization, a combination required a favorable vote by a majority of the members. Accordingly, I prepared a proxy statement for the members with a proxy card to be returned to management with the member's signature if the member did not intend to attend the meeting where a formal vote would be taken. The proxy cards returned were overwhelmingly in favor of the combination and authorized management to vote for the member.

The meeting drew a large crowd, and many members came forward and opposed the combination. They were cheered on by other members. I presided at the meeting. At one point, one of the members made a motion to postpone the meeting or something to that effect. I said we would have to vote on the motion and called for a recess while ballots were filled out, returned to the chair, and counted. I cast the vote of the people who had voted by proxy. When voting was complete and the votes counted, I announced the results. The motion was overwhelmingly defeated because proxy votes were many times the number of votes from those in attendance. We then voted to approve the combination.

Watching Radio Change

Radio has been a large part of my life both as a lawyer and as an investor. AM radio had been around for several years when I was born, and until the advent of television, it was the main source of home entertainment. People would sit around the radio and listen to many types of programming, including soap operas, quiz shows, situation comedies, mystery series, and children's shows. Among the popular programs were The Lone Ranger, The Green Hornet, Fibber McGee and Molly, and Let's Pretend. News was also popular, as was sports programming and even soap operas. Music was not nearly as prevalent on the radio as it is now. During the Great Depression, President Franklin Delano Roosevelt would use live radio for his fireside chats. The number and variety of programs broadcast were so large that John Dunning's massive *The Encyclopedia of Old-Time Radio* took up 745 pages to cover the period from the 1920s to the early 1960s.

Some of the sports programming was, to say the least, unusual. Bob Elson in Chicago would broadcast White Sox home games from the ballpark. But because of financial or other constraints, he broadcast away games from a studio in Chicago while he watched a telegraphic play out of what was taking place. He would add crowd noise when appropriate. Listeners could hear the telegraph's tick-tock and know when something new had happened.

Radio sets were fairly large because they relied on vacuum tubes, and some were floor models that took up considerable space. Most radio stations were locally owned, but many became affiliated with networks owned by NBC, CBS, or the Mutual Radio Network, a cooperative owned by its stations. Among the radio pioneers were the Italian Guglielmo Marconi, who developed wireless telegraphy, and David Sarnoff, who developed commercial radio as part of RCA's corporate strategy.

The Federal Communications Commission regulates radio stations under the Communications Act of 1934. The FCC issues licenses to stations for a fixed, renewable term. AM radio stations broadcast with a transmitter from an antenna system composed of a tower and copper radials, which are typically underground and run from the base of the tower to a distance that can be as long as the tower's height. Although not connected, they form a circle around the tower. Radio stations can broadcast over long distances, particularly at night. The FCC licenses a radio station to a specific frequency and power, expressed in watts. Typically, the lower the frequency and the greater the watts, the more powerful the signal. But, with a few exceptions, the FCC licensed a number of radio stations across the country to operate at the same frequency. To prevent these stations from interfering with each other, the FCC authorized a station to broadcast at a power in a specific pattern. To achieve this pattern, which can be different at night, some radio stations have two or more towers and ground systems. Some AM stations are required to reduce power between sunset and sunrise, and some stations, called daytimers, are not allowed to broadcast at all during that period. A few stations are licensed to an exclusive frequency at 50,000 watts and permitted to broadcast at that power 24 hours a day. These stations, called clear-channel stations, can be heard across many states at night.

Some locations have a few areas where towers can be located. One such location is Honolulu, where multiple stations use the same tower. Most AM stations have been around for many years, and their tower sites are located in outlying areas where land is less expensive, and there are no neighbors to complain about an unsightly tower. But in recent years, the tower sites of some stations have become more valuable than the station licenses.

For several years, radio and television occupied a large portion of the FCC's agenda and were more highly regulated. At one point, the FCC required radio stations whose license terms were about to expire to conduct a thorough assessment of the needs of the communities they served and to demonstrate in their renewal applications how those needs were being addressed in their programming. The ascertainment process was extensive and required the participation of owners and managers. It even led at least one person to set up a consulting business to assist with the ascertainment. To meet the programming requirement, some stations broadcast programs featuring local officials discussing community needs, but you would have had to listen between midnight Sunday evening and 9 am or so Sunday morning to hear them.

The FCC also would not allow any station to be sold for a profit less than three years after it was purchased and restricted the number of radio stations that any one owner could own. As we will see, that restriction did not last.

The development of FM radio is largely attributed to Edwin Armstrong, who, unfortunately, did not ultimately benefit financially from doing so and who ultimately committed suicide because he thought he was a failure. In technical terms, AM radio varied the amplitude of radio waves, giving its signal a wide reach but at the expense of quality. Armstrong varied the radio waves' frequency by creating Frequency Modulation, FM, resulting in a signal that had less static and a much better sound.

Armstrong persuaded the FCC to create an FM broadcast spectrum between 42 and 50 MHz and thereafter created an FM network. He was also involved in the manufacture of receivers that could pick up the FM broadcasts. Others in the radio industry who relied on AM were not pleased and lobbied the FCC to shift the FM band to higher frequencies. They were successful. The FCC allocated FM channels from 88 to 108 MHz and assigned the old band to different uses. This obsoleted all the FM receivers that had been used to hear Armstrong's FM and set back the growth of FM radio for several years.

Unlike AM stations, FM stations' towers are not part of the antenna. Instead, they are used to hold transmission equipment. Because FM, unlike AM, is line-of-sight, the taller the tower, the better. Some

FM towers are installed on top of mountains or skyscrapers. FM does not use a ground system.

My first visit to a radio station's studio was disappointing. I was driving to the studios of WRTH, an AM radio station in Wood River, Illinois, and listening to it. I pictured in my mind what the announcer would look like. Anyone with his great voice must be well-dressed, trim, and handsome. When I entered the building and looked into the on-air studio, I saw a semi-bald, overweight man slumped in his chair, microphone in hand. Today, if I looked into an on-air studio, I could well just see an empty chair with a computer screen blinking with references to music, commercials, and promotions.

WRTH was owned by Robert W. Sudbrink, who was known as Woody. Woody lived in Beardstown, Illinois, where he was in the insurance business. He became interested in radio after he wound up being the owner of a radio station in Beardstown. Woody investigated the engineering allocation of radio station frequencies and applied for a new station with relatively low power in Wood River, Illinois. His application was granted, and he subsequently returned to the Federal Communications Commission (FCC) for increased power, which he successfully obtained. The next thing anyone knew, WRTH was serving the Greater St. Louis market from Wood River, Illinois. As required, the studio remained in Wood River, but the station's sales office was located in St. Louis, where General Manager Harold W. Gore held forth.

Woody then relied on O.D. for engineering. Kost. O.D. was from the Beardstown area, with a slow drawl and a down-home appearance that, coupled with his being a farmer, masked the fact that he was an excellent broadcast engineer and exceptionally smart.

I did not know it then, but Woody and Hal were later to have a huge impact on my business life.

I was in the Wood River area because I had been asked by my partner, Charlie Davis, to represent Woody's company in the sale of WRTH to Avco. Although I had previously represented clients in business acquisitions, I had never been involved in a radio station transaction. As was the custom, the first draft of the purchase contract was prepared by the buyer's attorney. It was fortunate that the radio station purchase agreements contained unique language due to FCC rules I was not familiar with, and the buyer's attorney had prepared an excellent, basic agreement. There were still several provisions I found objectionable, particularly in the warranty section. After a couple of days of negotiations, we reached a final agreement. It was then up to Woody's FCC attorney, Michael Bader of Haley, Bader & Potts, to prepare the necessary filings to get the FCC's consent to the transfer of the FCC licenses to Avco.

Michael was an extraordinary person. Not only was he a brilliant lawyer, but he was also one of the most decent, warm people I have ever met. He was also very wealthy. When MCI Communications sought to compete with AT&T in the long-distance business, it faced the formidable and expensive task of dueling AT&T through numerous filings and hearings before the FCC. The legal fees would have been enormous. Michael agreed to take a significant portion of the fees in MCI stock. Ultimately, he was the largest individual stockholder of MCI and a member of its Board of Directors. MCI did very well financially, but ultimately made the mistake of merging with WorldCom, with disastrous consequences. Fortunately, Michael had sold most of his holdings before the merger, which only confirmed what a smart man he was.

The fact that Michael Bader represented Woody was indicative of one of Woody's principal strengths, the ability to get excellent people to work for or with him. We will see more of this later.

I do not recall the exact price that Woody received from Avco for WRTH, but it was a substantial sum at the time. Woody used the money to embark on one of the most ambitious and seemingly foolish projects at the time – the purchase of FM radio stations. At that time, FM was considered of little value – it was primarily used to broadcast classical music and was certainly not profitable. But Woody was aware of FM's potential because of its superior broadcast signal and the clear sound it could produce for music.

FCC rules at the time only permitted one person or entity to own a maximum of seven AMs and seven FMs. Woody set to work acquiring FM stations in Houston, Miami, Chicago, Cincinnati, Baltimore, Atlanta, and Milwaukee. He was able to buy them for ridiculously low prices. I represented him as an attorney in all but one or two of these purchases.

The purchase negotiations were some of the most interesting of my legal career. The Atlanta stations (Woody acquired both an FM and an AM) were owned by Bob Jones University. I went to the University and met with an official and his attorney, who was a former FBI agent. By this time, I was using a basic contract that drew on a good part of the Avco contract but also included language of my own. As was, and still is, typical in acquisition agreements, the contract included representations and warranties. Since Woody was not buying the stations because of their existing programming, there were no financial warranties, but there were warranties regarding the status of the FCC licenses and the condition of the tangible assets being acquired. The University and its attorney absolutely refused to make any warranties. When I would approach the warranties from a risk standpoint, they agreed with me that the University should be responsible if certain facts were not true. For example, they agreed with me that Woody should not bear the risk if the FCC licenses were not in good standing and could be revoked. I kept probing and finally found what was bothering them. They finally admitted that they were concerned that if they made a warranty and it turned out to be false, they would have lied and therefore have sinned.

The signed contract did not contain any warranties. But it did include a provision stating that if certain conditions (the subjects of the warranties) were not met, the University, as the seller, would be financially responsible.

Another negotiation, but it was hardly that, took place with Paul Brake, who owned an FM station in Miami and programmed it with music he liked. The meeting with Paul took place at his open-air facility on a waterway. He was not making money with the station, and his sole reluctance to sell stemmed from his love of his programming and the station's call letters, which had special significance to him.

Typically, I would meet with the principals and their attorneys at the seller's office to negotiate the acquisition terms. Usually, the price had already been agreed upon, but there were still economic terms to be settled. Woody seldom, if ever, accompanied me to these meetings. It gave him a huge advantage. When contentious issues arose, I would say that Mr. Sudbrink was adamant and would never agree to what the other side was requesting, and I could not either. In most instances, the other side ultimately gave in. In the few exceptions, I would call Woody and, after we had discussed the issue and concluded that we would have to live with it to get the deal, he would talk to the principal on the other side and say that I had not understood his position and that he was agreeable to what was being requested.

As he was acquiring his FMs, Woody had two important decisions to make – how would they be programmed and who would he get to manage them. One of the amazing things about Woody was that he was thoroughly wired into what was going on in the broadcast industry, even though he did not like to travel and did not travel very often. Using the telephone, he learned an incredible amount of information.

Somehow, he came to know Jim Schulke, who, with the company he owned, Stereo Radio Productions, was developing an Easy Listening format for FMs. In a very contentious negotiation that I was not involved in until the end, Woody agreed to use Schulke's programming on all of Woody's FMs. I was called in at the end to negotiate the contract between Woody and SRP. I did not know it at the time, but when the contract was signed, Jim asked Woody whether SRP could engage me and my firm as its attorneys. Woody said no because of the potential for conflict between the two, but told Jim he would tell him when that was no longer a significant problem.

Jim had very strong ideas about his format and how it should be used. His concept was "matched flow," meaning each song should naturally follow the one that preceded it. Jim's music genius, Phil Stout, would sometimes work several hours to get an hour of the right combination of music for the format. Ultimately, the music would be dubbed onto reels and sent to stations subscribing to SRP's format. The stations were told when to play a particular reel depending on the time of day. From time to time, new reels were sent out to replace those previously used.

Jim Schulke was also very strict about the technical details of how a station broadcast his format and what kind of non-intrusive commercial was appropriate for the mood that the music created. Schulke was a perfectionist who insisted that stations subscribing to his service operate with the best possible signal. Other radio stations at that time were using 78rpm records to play music on the air. The announcer would rewind the needle to the beginning of a song so it would play the song from the start whenever he pressed a lever. But Schulke used large reels of music tape. Stations would have two or more tapes and would play songs in sequence according to Schulke's instructions. Schulke's Beautiful Music was solely instrumental, and announcers, whose talk was kept to a minimum except for commercials, did not announce the names of the songs being played. There are various technical measures, such as compression, that a radio station can take to slightly alter the sound it broadcasts. Schulke was quite clear about which technical things were or were not to be used. Woody was very faithful in following Schulke's recommendations. And they worked at least at that time. Something similar to Schulke's Beautiful Music can be heard with Escape on Sirius.

With his great skill, Woody identified young people in the broadcast industry who had what he considered the most important attribute of a General Manager – great sales ability. He assembled a team of his General Managers and supporting personnel, who went on to become important players in the industry. The individuals included John Lauer, Brian Bieler, Dick Foreman, Neil Rockoff, Norm Feuer, and Dennis Ciapora. Al Gore remained with Woody and became the person who oversaw all of the stations' operations.

Woody was able to attract good people because he offered them the opportunity to make a great deal of money if the station they worked for was successful. We developed an employment agreement that provided a modest current salary but also called for phantom stock. Typically, the agreement had a five-year term and provided that the employee would receive a lump-sum amount at the end of the agreement equal to a percentage of the increase in the station's value during the term. The station was valued using a multiple of cash flow for the 12 months preceding the end of the contract's term. The phantom stock vested in increments throughout the term.

While Woody was negotiating to buy the FMs, he moved to Ft Lauderdale. Again demonstrating his ability to pick good people, Woody hired William McEntee, a young accountant from Arthur Andersen, to be his financial man. Bill was incredibly quick with numbers and exceptionally smart. The two of them prepared detailed projections of the FMs' financial operations over the next few years. The projections showed that the stations would operate at a loss for a period of some months but would then become increasingly profitable.

It was apparent that additional funds would be necessary to fund operations during the initial stages of unprofitability. At that time, I was doing legal work for venture capital firms and also had a good relationship with people at the First National Bank of Chicago. Accordingly, I took the projections and met with John Canning, who was then the head of the bank's venture capital fund. John and his people conducted their financial investigation and concluded that the project was too risky for them to get involved. Subsequently, the bank sold the fund to John and his people, who went on to become very successful. John became an extremely wealthy individual.

But the fund's turn-down was one of the best things that happened to Woody.

My law firm, Hopkins & Sutter, represented a community bank on the west side of Chicago at that time. One of my partners, Michael Phenner, had a good relationship with the bank's Chairman, who suggested I talk to him about securing a bank loan for Woody. This I did, and the bank agreed to make a loan on very favorable terms. Amazingly, a financing considered too risky for a venture capital company (which would have demanded equity kickers and high rates of return) was found appropriate for a bank loan at a reasonable interest rate.

Woody and his people went on to operate his seven FM stations with the SRP format and produced operating results that were amazingly consistent with the projections that Woody and Bill McEntee had prepared and provided to the venture capital company and the bank.

But the bank missed the best part. The manager of Woody's FM in Chicago, without talking to Woody, went to the bank's Chairman and insisted that the bank advertise on the station because it was getting Woody's banking business. The Chairman was furious and called Woody, telling him to get the loan out of the bank. Fortunately, this was easy because the stations now had positive cash flow, and it was relatively easy to move the loan to a bank in Atlanta.

After a few years of successful operation, Woody sold all his radio properties. He netted several million, but it is fair to say that his FMs were probably worth close to a billion in the early 2000s.

Eventually, Schulke asked me to represent him. He changed his company's name from Stereo Radio Productions to Schulke Radio Productions, and it was very successful with his "Beautiful Music" format. He reached an agreement with the BBC to obtain exclusive broadcast rights in the United States for music specially recorded for the BBC. It gave Jim an edge over his competitors, the chief one of which was Bonneville.

Jim used considerable research to determine which songs to play and when. The "Beautiful Music" format was all instrumentals. Schulke started a new format, called Schulke II, a mix of instrumentals and vocals that was somewhat more upbeat than the original.

I spent many hours on the phone with Schulke, not all of which were devoted to legal matters. Like other clients of my clients (including Sudbrink), Jim sometimes used me as a sounding board. I was used this way not because the clients thought I could answer questions, but because they did not want to share intimate business matters with their employees and needed someone to talk to about them. In each case, it seemed that they did not feel that the spouse could fulfill the same role. This changed dramatically with Sudbrink. He divorced his wife and married a woman he met walking on the beach. She resented his closeness to me and turned Woody against me. She also turned Woody against his children. After a few years, she died, and Woody reunited with his children and renewed his friendship with me.

Schulke's success caught the attention of Cox Communications, which was part of the Cox Media Empire headquartered in Atlanta. Cox purchased Jim's company for an amount that made Jim wealthy by the standards of the time.

But Cox's timing was not good. Schulke's music thrived when FM began to come alive with its superior signal for music. However, the music attracted an "older" audience – one which was not considered attractive by advertisers. Consequently, FM stations went with more upbeat music, ranging from current pop to jazz to country and western, and more. The Beautiful Music format had a rather quick demise.

After selling all his radio stations, Woody ventured into television, buying a UHF station in Atlanta and another in southern Illinois. At one point, he asked me to loan him money, which I found astonishing given the millions he had received from the sale of the stations. He persisted and said he would pay a very attractive interest rate. I succumbed. He repaid the principal but reneged on the interest.

The music played by radio stations was recorded on records and later on tapes and sold at music stores. There is no way the artists and recording studios were going to let radio stations play their music for free. Accordingly, syndicators were used to charge radio stations fees for playing the music. SESAC, BMI, and ASCAP performed this function depending on the artist. Even talk radio stations had to subscribe because if they played a commercial that included a licensed song, there was hell to pay.

Some stations were non-commercial, such as those affiliated with NPR (National Public Radio). The commercial stations depended on advertising to pay their bills and generate profits. With a few exceptions, such as ethnic stations, advertisers wanted to know enough listeners were hearing their ads to make the ad purchase worthwhile. The solution was Arbitron, which measured listenership. It would assemble a representative group of people and measure what they listened to and when during a rating period. It would then issue ratings ranking the stations by listenership. Arbitron ratings were critical for many stations. Some would try various tactics, like contests during the rating period, to influence ratings, but if they got too blatant, Arbitron would call them out. Some music syndicators for FM stations began using focus groups to ensure the music they offered would attract listeners.

If a station's overall Arbitron rating was not great, there still was hope. Arbitron's report, which stations had to pay for, contained demographic information and also showed listenership by day parts. So a station could brag that it ranked highly, for example, among young women, and then seek out advertisers who sell products or services to those women.

The types of formats broadcast on FM expanded beyond Schulke's beautiful music format. Current pop, rock, and country became popular, as did jazz. Classical music was typically broadcast only on a non-commercial station. Some disk jockeys became very popular and usually would broadcast during "drive time."

As FM became more popular, AM listenership declined, and AM stations began broadcasting more talk programs. Talk radio was hampered for several years by the FCC's Fairness Doctrine. According to a report by the Congressional Research Service:

> "The Fairness Doctrine consisted of two basic requirements:
>
> 1. That every licensee devotes a reasonable portion of broadcast time to the discussion of controversial issues or public importance; and
>
> 2. That in doing so, [the broadcaster must be] fair – that is, [the broadcaster] must affirmatively endeavor to make facilities available for the expression of contrasting viewpoints held by responsible elements with respect to the controversial issues presented.

The validity of the Fairness Doctrine came before the United States Supreme Court in 1969 in *Red Lion Broadcasting Co., Inc. v Federal Communications Commission.* The case involved charges broadcast by Reverend Billy James Hargis on a Pennsylvania radio station. He described an author as having been fired for, among other things, having worked for a Communist-affiliated publication, having defended Alger Hiss, and having attacked J. Edgar Hoover. The author demanded a reply time, but the station refused. The FCC found that the station had failed to meet its obligations under the Fairness Doctrine, and the Supreme Court ultimately upheld the FCC's decision, finding the Fairness Doctrine constitutional.

But the Doctrine continued to be questioned and was repealed by the FCC in 1987. One can speculate what cable channels FOX News, MSNBC, and CNN would be like if the Fairness Doctrine were applied to them. But it is unlikely that it would have been applied to them even if the FCC had not repealed it, because they are cable channels, not broadcast stations.

Another FCC radio requirement, fortunately repealed, was the Primer on Ascertainment of Community Problems. The Primer required radio stations filing for the renewal of their licenses to spend considerable time ascertaining community needs, including, among other things, conducting interviews with significant community groups. The station then had to propose programming to address the community's needs and problems. The interviews and other work required for the proposal took considerable time. Some radio stations hired one person to perform the ascertainment. The FCC didn't say when the programming should air, and it was frequently heard in the wee hours of Sunday morning.

After Sudbrink sold all his radio stations, I began a partnership with Harold W. Gore. He was an experienced broadcaster, which I was not. Hal had started as a radio salesperson, had become the general manager of Sudbrink's station in St. Louis, and then had been the group manager of Sudbrink's seven commercial FM stations. Gore was very smart and very knowledgeable and had owned religious AM stations. Our first radio station was WRTH, an AM licensed to Camden, New Jersey, that covered the Greater Philadelphia area. It had a religious format. Most of the broadcast day featured pastors who purchased either a quarter or a half hour to do their own show, which was submitted on tape. Invariably, they asked for contributions, and it was quite clear they monitored the source of their contributions to determine whether it was profitable to be on our station. Apparently, they found that it was because they stayed. One of the programs featured sermons and donation requests from a pastor who had died several months earlier.

Gore had some interesting stories to tell about religious broadcasters. He said that when they had a conference, the hotel bar was empty, but room service was swamped. One story he told I found hard to believe. He said one religious broadcaster announced that if people sent him contributions, they would receive a personally autographed photo of Jesus Christ. Gore enjoyed a good life. At one point, he partnered with the general manager of one of Sudbrink's FMs to buy a storm window company. The company obtained a significant bank loan that Gore fully guaranteed, even though he held a minority interest. The company failed, and the bank pursued Gore for the full amount because his partner had very limited funds. I worked with Hal to negotiate an arrangement that would substantially reduce the total amount he would be liable for. The remaining amount was still substantial, and I loaned Hal enough money to cover it.

Hal and I purchased other radio stations with the idea of having them broadcast religious programming. We bought AMs in Scranton and Warren, Pennsylvania, but found it extraordinarily difficult to convert them to new religious stations. But we were able to sell them for little or no loss. The same thing happened with a station we purchased in Louisville, Kentucky, which had a much better signal than the existing religious station in the area. But neither the preachers nor the listeners were interested in converting. Fortunately, we sold that station for a small profit.

At some point, we borrowed money from Philadelphia National Bank, which we agreed to repay in installments. But in the 1980s, the Federal Reserve, under the Chairmanship of Paul Volcker, raised the Fed Funds rate to nearly 20%. The interest rate on our loan was tied to Prime, and it increased substantially. The bank insisted I come in to discuss our loan and insisted that we pay it off. "We are paying interest," I said. "Are all your other borrowers able to do that?" That did not satisfy the bank. A few days later, I was listening to the radio in my car and heard a commercial from a local Chicago-area bank, Cole Taylor, encouraging people to do business with it. I called the bank, and within days, we borrowed from Cole Taylor and paid off Philadelphia National Bank. It began a great relationship.

WTMR was profitable, and we sold it to a group owner who had other stations, both religious and secular. We planned to take advantage of the Internal Revenue Code's like-kind exchange provisions. We acquired WROD-AM with an oldies format in the Daytona Beach, Florida, market, and KIRV, which broadcast a religious format in Fresno, California, where we had previously acquired KBIF.

Subsequently, we acquired additional AM stations in Florida that, in addition to the Daytona Beach station, were ultimately sold. Amazingly, we were able to sell for little to no gain or loss.

Hispanic religion has also had success on the radio. With the help of Linda Johnson Hayes, a brilliant woman in California, we were able to purchase an AM station in Phoenix and lease it to a Hispanic pastor who had a small network of Hispanic religious stations. We subsequently purchased an AM station in Bakersfield, California, and, with Linda's help, converted it to a Hispanic religious format. We were surprised by how well it did from the beginning, but it ultimately leveled off, and we sold it to the pastor on our Phoenix station. The Phoenix station was ultimately sold to a Catholic group that programmed it for the Catholic religion.

Another area where AM radio became successful is ethnic broadcasting. It was particularly true in the Los Angeles area, where stations were very successful in programming for Asians. We ventured into that area when, in the 1990s, we purchased KBIF, a radio station in Fresno, California, that broadcast to a variety of listeners, including

Hmong. Many Hmongs lived in Laos and were recruited by the CIA to fight the Viet Cong during the Vietnam War. The Hmongs were tough fighters and fought the Viet Cong vigorously. When the United States withdrew from Vietnam, it brought thousands of Hmong to the United States, where many settled in Fresno, the Twin Cities area, and Milwaukee. We broadcast for the Hmongs Monday through Friday and for Punjabis on Saturday and Sunday. To keep up with changing times, KBIF's programming was available on an app, and KBIF also had programming on Facebook.

Talk radio thrived after the demise of the Fairness Doctrine, featuring Rush Limbaugh and other conservative broadcasters. Efforts to program talk radio with more liberal voices were unsuccessful because they could not attract sufficient listeners. Not every conservative voice was successful on the radio. Former Governor Huckabee started a syndicated radio show, and we signed up for it with our second AM in Fresno, California. It bombed and was cancelled.

As noted above, Sudbrink had to deal with FCC rules limiting the number of radio stations that one owner could own. Over time, the FCC relaxed the ownership rules and eventually dropped them entirely, except for a limit on the number of stations that could be owned in a single market. The lifting of the station ownership limitation sparked an explosion of radio station acquisitions and led to the creation of large radio group owners. The FCC was quite liberal in interpreting the number of stations in a market and included non-commercial stations.

Two such group owners were Clear Channel Communications and Cumulus Media, Inc., both of which became involved with private equity and other firms and purchased dozens of radio stations. They both ultimately went through bankruptcy proceedings, with Clear Channel eventually becoming iHeartMedia.

A major technical change took place with the emergence of internet radio. Internet radio stations are online audio streams that can be accessed through websites or apps. iHeartMedia now boasts of owning 860 radio stations in 160 US markets. Internet radio stations can be heard anywhere with an internet connection and do not require towers.

One group that has not fared well with radio stations is employees. Yes, some people have made enormous amounts, such as Rush Limbaugh and high-profile music disc jockeys. But many employees have not done well. This includes some who had important positions, such as station managers. The station managers I knew did not have any retirement plan, and because of changing station ownership, they worked for many different companies during their broadcast careers. One of them, who was in retirement, could not afford to travel a few hundred miles to attend the funeral of a very close broadcasting friend. He was in the process of arranging a reverse mortgage to survive. People in the broadcast industry are aware of the problem and have formed the Broadcasters Foundation to raise funds to help retired broadcasters who are now in dire economic straits. But that can only do so much.

Obviously, the radio landscape has changed. Radio will continue to be an important communication medium, but it will never be as popular as it was in the 60s, 70s, and 80s.

The Cable Television Experience

My involvement with Sudbrink led me to get into an entirely new business – cable television. Sudbrink used a media broker named Bill Kepper to help Sudbrink find FM stations to buy. Kepper lived in Evanston, where I lived. One time when I was on a flight with Kepper, he told me that the radio was great, but cable television would be even better. He said he had a company building a new cable television system in a small town in Illinois and was looking for investors. I agreed to invest a small amount that I cannot remember. Months went by, and Kepper came back to me with a new offer. He was forming a new company to purchase a cable system in Belvidere, Illinois, and to build new cable systems in towns just south of the Wisconsin–Illinois border. Among these towns were Harvard, Woodstock, and McHenry, as well as the unincorporated areas in between. This looked more interesting to me, so I agreed to invest in it and to also offer it to some of my legal clients, including Sudbrink.

As I recall, Sudbrink and Alan Cummings invested in the new company that I think was called Lake County Cablevision. Because of my and my clients' investments, I became a director and met from time to time with Kepper to discuss obtaining cable television franchises from the towns and planning construction. These meetings typically took place in McHenry, which was several miles from Evanston. They typically were held at night, so it made for a long night. The company obtained a franchise for Harvard, and the time came to arrange for the cable systems to be constructed. Kepper wanted the company to adopt a new cable-construction system that offered new opportunities. After much discussion, we reached an impasse. I said that we were too small a company to use a new construction system, and I did not want us to be "the new kid on the block." We couldn't agree, so we decided to split the company into two. I would take the existing Belvidere cable system, as well as the franchise for Harvard, where no system had yet been built.

As I drove home from the meeting, I said to myself, "What am I doing? How can I run a company?" It turned out I was helped by the same thing that greatly helped Sudbrink – finding exceptional people. In this case, it was Don Arndt and his son. Arndt worked as a salesman for a company that sold equipment for cable television companies. He lived in Lake Geneva, Wisconsin, and was very knowledgeable about the cable industry. With his help, we hired a company that built cable systems.

The cable industry at that time was not in major market areas but in the "boon docks." Its function was to erect large towers capable of capturing signals from major market off-air television stations. The company would receive the signals, transmit them over cables, and then deliver them to individual homes. They were blessed with government rules that required telephone companies to allow cable to be installed on the telephone companies' poles at a small cost.

Since I learned of the cable television investment through my legal work, I felt it was a partnership opportunity that required me to offer my partners the chance to invest in the new company – Community Cablevision, Inc. Only three or four participated. I told them that they should not expect any return for months, if not years.

Most cable systems at the time offered only 12 channels. We decided to offer 35 which included a local municipal channel and e news channel that consisted of teletype messaging. This, of course, was in addition to the off-the-air TV stations we were able to pick up from Chicago. A key question we faced was the amount we would charge cable customers. It came down to two considerations. If you charge too little, many people would not think it was worth subscribing to. Alternatively, if you charged too much, many people would think it was too expensive. We decided to charge $10.50 a month plus $2 for the monthly rental of a box that would take the cable channels and convert them into signals that would appear as programs on their TVs. People could purchase the cable boxes for $10, but few did.

With only the cable system in Belvidere and the franchise in Harvard, I decided to look for other possibilities. The most likely was Walworth, Wisconsin, which is straight up the road from Harvard. To build a cable system in a village or town, you had to have a franchise approved by the village or town's board of supervisors. Franchises typically had a 15-year term and provided for the village or town to receive 3% of basic cable revenue. I was able to get an appointment before an evening meeting of the Walworth supervisors. But they were very suspicious about what I was offering and turned me down.

Stymied, I then decided to approach the Village of Fontana, which is located next to Walworth. When I met with the Fontana supervisors, they listened carefully and then one of them, a businessman, said:

"It won't cost us anything. In fact, the village will generate revenue, and our residents will have access to better television. Why wouldn't we want this?"

With that, the supervisors voted to approve the franchise. This "broke the dam." It wasn't long before Walworth decided it wanted cable, also, and cable was approved by a township along Lake Geneva east of Fontana. The biggest challenge became the Village of Williams Bay, which is on the other side of the lake. A media company in Milwaukee was involved with Williams Bay, and it seemed all but certain that that company would get the franchise. But it didn't apply, and we also got Williams Bay. We were able to serve all these communities from a tower we built in Harvard. Fortunately, we were able to run cable along the telephone company poles from Harvard to the Wisconsin communities.

We were challenged by the little town of Sharon, which is situated all by itself, a few miles from the north-south road that carried our cable. We finally capitulated and built a tower just for Sharon.

We did not need any salespeople. Cable sold itself, and it wasn't long before we were profitable and able to pay some of our bank debt. We established an office in Walworth to handle billing and collect payments. We did need someone to pay the bills and our employees. At the time, Gail and I were living in Evanston in a house with a somewhat isolated second-floor room at the end of a hallway. I set this up as an office and put an ad in the local paper for office help. I interviewed an older lady who seemed perfect for the job. We hired her, then discovered that she could use only one arm. But it turned out not to be a problem because she did all the work necessary.

Every weekend, Gail and I would drive up from Evanston to visit the office and the workers. Our drive took us through Richmond, Illinois, and Genoa City, Wisconsin, which were next to each other on the Illinois-Wisconsin border. Being opportunistic, it wasn't long before we received franchises and built cable systems in both towns, with a tower we built in Genoa City. We soon added Twin Lakes, Wisconsin.

As time went on, we began providing cable channels, including CNN and other national content, from satellite dishes at our tower sites.

The cable industry began having national conferences that offered great food and drinks and good lectures. I will never forget a conference where I got into a discussion about the number of channels cable systems should offer. I said, "Thirty-five channels should be more than adequate for everybody." The executive of a large national cable company looked at me and strongly disagreed. It turned out he was right, and I was naïve. As we well know now, people don't watch the same channels, so the number of available channels on cable and satellite is huge.

We were doing well. The number of subscribers was growing, and Don Arndt's son, Donnie, as a full-time employee, was doing a great job managing the installation of cable to people's homes. But two developments were challenging. The first was that cable systems were selling local advertising. For us to do that would have required investing in more people and more equipment. The second was programming costs. Channels such as CNN and others charged subscription fees for providing programming to their subscribers, and we were at a significant disadvantage. The large national cable companies could negotiate good rates, but our bargaining position was poor.

The problems small operators such as Community Cablevision faced did not go unnoticed by media brokers and others in the cable industry. One day, I met in my office at Hopkins and Sutter with a man who presented himself as a cable system broker. His name was Bruce Falkenberg, and he was very impressive. After careful consideration and discussion with others, we decided to sell our company, which we did. We sold to TCI, a company that was then of medium size in the industry. The contract was signed by John Malone, who is now worth billions.

Fortunately, all our investors made nice profits with a couple of exceptions. As I mentioned earlier, I gave my law partners the opportunity to invest in Community Cablevision and told them that they should not expect a return for several months and maybe even a few years. A couple of them grew impatient, so we bought them out early. They made little if any return on their investment. We allowed Don Arndt and his son to invest in a radio deal, and, fortunately, they made a profit.

I got to know Bruce Falkenberg very well. It turned out that we were his first cable television deal, which came as a big surprise to me. Bruce started referring me legal business, and I provided legal assistance to some of the groups he represented. At one point, I represented his company. I will never forget one opportunity he provided for me - to represent Ketchikan, Alaska, which owned the local telephone company and was considering selling it. Unfortunately, our visit to the town was in winter, and it was bitterly cold. Our plane landed on an island, and we had to get a ferry to reach the village. It was cold waiting for the ferry. To make matters worse, Ketchikan decided not to sell the telephone company.

Watching Newspapers Change

One of the two lengthy involvements I had with Hopkin & Sutter clients was with a family in Kankakee. Originally, there was one company, run by two brothers who were grandsons of an Illinois governor. One brother, Burrell Small, was primarily interested in broadcasting and cable television. The other brother, Len Small, was primarily interested in newspaper publishing. Our firm was consulted about a way to split the company into two, with each brother winding up with a company that was in his favorite business. This was accomplished, and I wound up being the firm's representative of both companies. Len Small was more active. He was the publisher of The Kankakee Daily Journal and soon had me represent Small Newspaper Group ("SNG") in acquisitions of newspapers in Rochester, Minnesota. And Moline, Illinois. This was in addition to the newspapers SNG already owned in Ottawa, Illinois, and LaPorte, Indiana.

Len also joined with three other newspaper owners in purchasing Family Weekly, a Sunday newspaper supplement like Parade Magazine. The four executives were brilliant, and I was pleased to represent Family Weekly and listen to their discussions. As time went on, they decided to sell Family Weekly. The sale negotiations were held in New York. I believe the buyer was CBS. At one point during the negotiations, a sticking point emerged. We knew that the head of CBS really wanted Family Weekly. So, I said that the sellers would be more receptive if you increased the price. The price was increased, and the sale was closed. Later, when I told Len what our fee would be, he said, "Cordy, that's not enough. You need to charge more." So, I did.

Len and I became good friends. He was very active in the newspaper industry, and he and his wife, Jean Alice, were good friends with Katherine Graham, the Publisher of the Washington Post.

Because of the distance between the newspapers' locations, SNG owned a single-engine airplane and had a pilot on its staff. Every time the pilot left me off at an airport after a trip, he would say, "Now comes the dangerous part of your trip."

Len was elected President of the Newspaper Publishers Association. But when he was being driven from Kankakee to O'Hare airport in Chicago for the beginning of his service, he was killed when a truck went through a stop sign and crashed into the passenger side of the car. It was devastating.

Jean Alice became more active with the newspapers. She had a strong interest in the editorial content of the papers, particularly the Kankakee Daily Journal. She and I had a very good relationship, and I became a director of SNG. Meanwhile, Rob Small, one of Len and Jean Alice's three children, became President. Rob had divorced his wife and married a woman who lived in France and owned a castle. Gail and I went to Paris for the wedding.

Jean Alice arranged for SNG to acquire two newspapers in California, one of which was managed by Tom Small. She was also responsible for the construction of a new facility at the Rochester paper for printing presses.

In the 1980s, I was engaged by two men, Douglas Ruhe and William Geissler, to represent them in their efforts to develop subscription TV stations. Both were followers of the Baha'i religion. They were bright and very ambitious. At one point, Ruhe learned that United Press International was for sale. UPI was a major competitor of the Associated Press. AP differed from UPI in that it was owned by existing newspapers and got most of its stories from their newspapers, which were distributed to all the newspaper owners. By contrast, UPI was owned by a single corporation. According to an article in the Tennessean, UPI had "some 7,500 clients around the world, maintains a staff of more than 2,000 employees working out of 224 bureaus."

Ruhe persisted in his efforts to acquire UPI and learned that it would not require substantial funds to do so. In fact, it could be acquired for nothing. Ironically, the owner, Scripps Howard, would be better off not being the owner of UPI. I persuaded Ruhe and Geissler that their chances would be better if they had partners who were known in the journalism industry. They agreed, and I reached out to Jean Alice and a broadcasting client, Robert W. ("Woody") Sudbrink, about the possibility of joining in the acquisition. They initially agreed but, after learning more about the risks involved, declined to participate. I talked to Rob Small about getting involved. The Tennessean described his reaction as follows:

"When Cordy Overgaard called me," Small said, "he told me he thought that the chances to save UPI were too slim and none. But he told me that these two men he knew were very smart and creative."

Details about the acquisition of UPI are covered in considerable detail in the book Down To The Wire – UPI's Fight for Survival by Gregory Gordon and Ronald E Cohen.

I flew to New York for several weeks, but Rob and I were unable to get Ruhe and Geisler to take steps that were critically needed. They were bound and determined to do their own thing.

There was one experience I will never forget. Shortly after it was publicly announced that our group had acquired UPI, we met with Abe Rosenthal of the New York Times. Described by Gordon and Cohen as "the most powerful man on the world's most powerful newspaper.... Rosenthal, blunt and caustic, skipped the usual pleasantries." Indeed, he did. He demanded to know what our group had paid for UPI. Ruhe was anything but intimidated and told Rosenthal that, just as the New York Times had not disclosed what it paid for businesses it acquired, UPI would not either. Rosenthal became furious and virtually kicked us out of his office.

Small, and I finally decided it was hopeless and withdrew from UPI. It went through various phases thereafter, but finally went into bankruptcy.

After Len's death, I became a director of Small Newspaper Group. After Jean Alice's death and my retirement from Hopkins &

Sutter, I became a Vice President of the corporation and a part-time consultant. Ultimately, I was in charge of digital at a time when newspapers were beginning the key transition from print to digital. It was made difficult by the reluctance of many newspaper people to accept what was happening. Rob and I began having differences because I thought he was not managing the newspapers in the group as he should have, and was not holding the publishers accountable for their actions or failure to act. So I resigned not only from my positions with the corporation but also from my role as a trustee of the trust that controlled the corporation. As happened with many newspaper companies, the corporation began shedding newspapers.

As previously mentioned, my first involvement in the newspaper business was as a paperboy, delivering newspapers when they were very popular. When I first visited a newspaper facility, some of the paper was produced with hot type. The front page of newspapers changed dramatically over the years. The front pages of the first newspapers I worked with had columns of text with no photos. As time went on, photos became more prevalent, and many were in color and took up considerable space.

I was in Kankakee at the Daily Journal's facility on September 15, 1982, when it received the first satellite-delivered paper - USA Today, the first national paper. It was the brainchild of Allen Neuharth of Gannett, a good friend of Jean Alice Small. Its circulation eventually reached over two million.

A key newspaper revenue source was classified ads, and, as MINNPOST described, this "golden goose" was killed by Craigslist.

"Those little three-and five-line ads were a license to print money. And didn't require much of an investment in salesmanship. People actually called to place their ads – all the papers had to do was answer the phone and take the order. At $10, $15, or $20 a pop, multiplied by thousands of ads per day, the money poured in."

According to MINNPOST:

"Newspaper classified advertising peaked in 2000 at $19.6 billion. In 2012, the most recent year for which data are available from the Newspaper Association of America, classified advertising was $4.6 billion - a drop of about 77 percent in barely more than a decade."

Of course, classified advertising subsequently dropped much more. But the real culprit for newspapers has been the internet. A January 30, 2024, New York Times article with the headline, "A Grim Look at the State of the News," put it this way:

"[T]he mainstream news industry – once the de facto watchdog and facilitator of public discourse – is struggling to stay afloat …. An average of five local newspapers are closing every two weeks according to Northwestern University's Medill School…"

The article points out that The New York Times, The New Yorker, and The Boston Globe have succeeded by attracting digital subscribers, while The Washington Post and The Los Angeles Times have been less successful. The major network television companies have also suffered, losing viewers and, in several cases, reducing staff.

This points to a major problem today. Many people are not getting any news, while others are getting it from a variety of sources, some of which provide questionable or slanted news. More about this later.

The Steve Small Kidnapping

I did much less work for the Burrell Small side of the family, which was involved in radio broadcasting and cable television. I represented them in the sale of one or more of their properties and maintained a good relationship with the family members.

Steve Small, Burrell's son, was using family funds to restore a Frank Lloyd Wright building in Kankakee. One night at about 1 am on September 2, 1987, I received a call from Steve's brother-in-law. He told me that Steve called him and said he had received a call from someone who said he was a policeman and that there had been a burglary at the Frank Lloyd Wright building and that when he went out his back door, a man accosted him and kidnapped him. Steve said, "Call Cordy. But don't call the police."

I put the phone down and called the FBI immediately. FBI agents went to Small's home and met with his wife, Nancy. Thereafter, the kidnapper, a man named Danny Edwards, made more calls and demanded a ransom of One Million Dollars in cash. The FBI planned to have one of their agents impersonate me and meet with the kidnapper. Edwards made calls from several pay phones, and the FBI apparently traced them and identified Edwards as a suspect. He and his girlfriend, Nancy Rish, were arrested. Both denied having anything to do with the kidnapping.

For whatever reason, at one point, Edwards said, "We'd better hurry," and led the FBI agents to a wooded area where he had buried Steve in a wooden box. He had placed a tube from the box to the surface so Steve could breathe. But the tube was too small, and Steve had suffocated.

Because the case against Edwards was unique to Kankakee County, a special prosecutor from Cook County was appointed to try it. My recollection is that I was involved in this process. The special prosecutor, Michael Ficaro, became a trial lawyer at Hopkins & Sutter after the trial.

Edwards had confessed to the kidnapping, so the key question at the trial was what the penalty would be. The jury had been selected in Rockford and brought to Kankakee for the trial. The jury found Edwards guilty and eligible for the death penalty, which is what he received.

Nancy Rish was tried separately. She claimed she was unaware of what Edwards was doing. But because she was connected to things such as the construction of the wooden box that Small was put in, as well as her presence with Edwards when he made calls that led the jury to find her guilty. She was given two sentences – a life sentence and a 30-year term.

I was present in Kankakee in the days following the kidnapping. The Small's home was located on a block with an alley. Across the alley was the home of George Ryan, then the Illinois Lieutenant Governor. I met with Ryan at his home, where he told me he oversaw the Illinois

State Police's participation. Their instructions basically were to do what the FBI wanted. Ryan knew the Small family extremely well. It came as a shock to me and to many others when, on January 11, 2003, Ryan commuted Edward's death sentence. Ryan had served as Illinois Secretary of State, served two terms as Lieutenant Governor and was elected Illinois Governor. But things did not end well for Ryan. In December 2003, he was indicted for several federal charges and ultimately was convicted and sent to prison.

China

To say that China is unique is an understatement. It has gone through several different political and economic periods. One period involved two Opium Wars between Great Britain and China, during which Britain occupied Shanghai for a time. During my visit to Shanghai, I was surprised to see a building that the British had built.

A major development in China occurred in 1976, when Mao Zedong launched the Cultural Revolution. This was a dismal period in China. Many people were killed, and many people in large cities were forced to move to rural areas. Attacks were made based on people's culture, habits, and customs. For all practical purposes, China was closed to the World during the Cultural Revolution.

It is surprising, then, that President Nixon and Henry Kissinger visited China during the Cultural Revolution. Their visit did not end the revolution, nor did it lead to the opening up of China. During the visit, Nixon agreed to support the One China Policy – "there is but one China and Taiwan is part of China." The policy has received more attention in recent years as Taiwan has become a major chip developer.

The Cultural Revolution ended in 1989, and Deng Xiaoping came to power. He was responsible for the "opening up" and began a massive overhaul of China's infrastructure and political system.

Gail and I were on one of the first cruise ships to dock in China after its opening. We were bused to Beijing, and it felt as though we had gone back several years. There were very few cars and many bicycles. We were taken to the Great Hall of China, where we met with some Chinese officials in a small meeting room. It was followed by dinner in another room in the Great Hall, during which we were serenaded by a band that played Home on the Range. The next day, we were taken to the Great Wall, where we had the opportunity to walk along it for a while. The Chinese people were exceptionally friendly.

We next flew on a small public passenger plane to Xian, where we saw the amazing Terracotta Warriors. These are clay figures of soldiers, horses, chariots, and more, part of an underground metropolis that was not discovered until 1974. The metropolis was created at the order of Qin Shi Huangdi, who is said to have been the first Chinese emperor. We had to descend a few feet to a point where we could see the warriors. There are hundreds, perhaps thousands of them, and it is said that no two look alike. They were dark brown when we saw them, but we were told they had originally worn colorful uniforms. The horses and chariots were life-sized and very attractive. The area we saw, which was really called a pit, is one of many pits and the tomb of Qin Shi Huangdi. Excavation is still going on, and the tomb has not been opened. One report I read said that there is fear that it is booby trapped. There is also concern about substantial amounts of mercury in the area. One report said that Huangdi liked mercury with his wine.

Gail and I left China with very good feelings about the Chinese people we met.

I returned to China on personal business trips a few years later. I was accompanied by Doris Cheng, a Chinese woman I had met in Chicago. Her family had left Shanghai during the Cultural Revolution. After the opening, the Chinese government sent some of its officials to take courses at the Massachusetts Institute of Technology, and she met them when she was a student there. This enabled us to meet with some Chinese officials when we were in China. One of the officials we met with oversaw Township Enterprises. I and, like many people in the United States, did not look upon China at that time as much of a business country. We were wrong. Non-state-owned businesses in townships and villages were responsible for an increasing share of business output. I asked the official if any of the Township Enterprises would be interested in investment from the United States. He said he thought they would be. When Doris and I got back to the United States, we went to New York City and visited with a couple of investment companies. Almost disdainfully, they said they would not be.

Four years after the opening-up, many young Chinese enrolled in colleges and universities in the United States. Somewhat later, young people in the United States went to China for studies and internships. My grandson Andy Radelet is one such person who now speaks Mandarin.

From a low base, China has dramatically increased its standing in the world economy. It has made numerous investments in other countries. In 2013, Chairman XI launched a Belt and Road Initiative to invest in other countries and develop infrastructure projects involving Chinese firms and expertise. It has grown substantially.

A World Bank study found that China's 2024 global manufacturing output was 31.6% compared to 15.9% for the United States. One startling fact about China is its huge high-speed rail system. This compares to the United States, which is having difficulty building its first high-speed train system in California. China accounts for over 70% of the World's electric vehicle production. China clearly is the World's leading industrial company.

China has also been a major advocate of measures to address climate change. It has an 80% share of the solar panel market.

Not everything is perfect in China. It does have some problems with its economy. But it has one key advantage. A central government without the restraints present in the United States.

Social Media

As newspaper readership has declined, people are increasingly getting their news on social media. According to Pew Research, "about half of U.S. adults (53%) say they at least some times get news from social media…"

According to Pew Research, "38% of U.S. adults say they regularly get news on Facebook, and 35% say the same about YouTube." Currently, people 49 and younger are the biggest users of social media. Podcasts are becoming more common.

The key question social media presents is whether it is a reliable news source. According to Lumen:

"In 2020, Pew Research Center reported that Americans who primarily use social media for political news are less likely to have knowledge on a wide range of topics and issues in the news and more likely to have knowledge about false and unproven claims."

It would seem that most news is not conducive to social media. This is the case with live events, such as an airplane crash or a speech by an important business or government figure. A further issue is the reliability of information on social media. The website allsides.com has media bias charts that determine the level of bias of a new source.

In 2023, UNESCO and Ipsos issued a report on their Global Survey on the Impact of Online Disinformation and Hate Speech. The survey revealed that, on average, 56% of internet users across 16 countries frequently use social media to stay updated on current events, with the United States at 37%.

The survey reported that "Across all 16 countries, 68% of internet users told us that social media is the place where disinformation is most widespread, far ahead of groups on online messaging apps (38%) and media websites/apps (20%). This sentiment is overwhelmingly prevalent in all countries, age groups, social backgrounds, and political preferences. This is even more important, as citizens feel that disinformation is a real threat: 85% express concern about its impact and influence on their fellow citizens, a figure that reaches 88% in countries with high HDI and 90% in those with medium/low HDI. They are even more inclined 87% to believe this phenomenon has already had a major impact on the political life of their country."

This is very scary!

Artificial Intelligence

Artificial Intelligence AI is very much in the news now, but it is not a new development. It has been developing over several decades. AI has at least three major ramifications:

First, it is responsible for substantial investment in new facilities. Facilities that require massive construction and development funds, as well as ongoing new energy demands.

Second, robots and other factors substantially reduce the need for human workers, thereby increasing unemployment.

Third, it will greatly increase wealth and income inequality.

In a column, Jim VandeHei and Mike Allen, founders of Axios, said this:

"Bad news: The U.S. government, even if it weren't shut down, is doing nothing to prepare Americans for the coming, in some areas already unfolding, economic and jobs shock."

***

Elon Musk, an AI architect and optimist, and Sanders, an AI skeptic, agree about little. But both are warning that AI-powered robots could soon take so many jobs, America might need to pay U.S. workers *not* to work."

The depressing future they project will not happen overnight, but it will gradually be felt in the months ahead. A key question is the extent to which the impact of AI will differ in the United States and China, and what that difference will mean.

Income and Wealth Inequality

The question, of course, is not whether there is income and wealth inequality but whether it has increased.

The word being heard frequently today is **affordability**.

More and more people in the US are living day to day and are very concerned about their ability to survive. An October 2024 Congressional Budget Office report said this:

"Over those 33 years, family wealth was unevenly distributed, and inequality increased. In 2022, families in the top 10 percent of the distribution held 60 percent of all wealth, up from 56 percent in 1989, and families in the top 1 percent of the distribution held 27 percent, up from 23 percent in 1989. The share of wealth held by the rest of the families in the top half of the distribution shrank from 37% to 33% over the same period. Families in the bottom half of the distribution held 6% of all wealth in both 1989 and 2022."

When I was practicing Law, I represented public corporations, and the ratio between what the top executives received and what the average worker received did not seem out of line. But according to Income Inequality.org, this has changed.

"According to Office of Management and Budget data and Economic Policy Research, when corporate tax receipts made up 21.8 percent of all revenue in 1965, the average CEO -to median- worker pay ratio was 21 to 1. By 2019, corporate tax receipts had fallen to just 6.6 percent of federal revenue, and the average pay ratio had risen to 230 to 1."

Neither Harris nor Trump really addressed the income inequality issue during the campaign. Only 39% of voters said Kamala Harris had the best approach compared with 32% who said Trump did. Biden did not address this issue either during his Presidency, which may explain why his favorability was so low. Neither party is addressing the issue now. It will be an even bigger issue in primaries and elections going forward.

So what should be done?

Over ten years ago, Joseph E. Stiglitz, who won the Nobel Prize in economics, wrote **The Price of Inequality**, in which he made several suggestions for changes to address inequality. They included having a more progressive income and corporate tax system and a more effective estate tax system. According to Walter Klowers, the top marginal income tax rate dropped from 70% in 1965 to 37% in 2022. During the same period, the maximum capital gains tax for individuals and corporations declined from 25% to 21%.

Unfortunately, given the lack of accountability of our elected officials, it would be shocking if any of his suggestions are adopted.

The Broken US Political System

I believe the United States political system is broken. This is primarily due to three factors: a faulty constitution, money, and Supreme Court decisions.

Faulty Constitution: The Constitution provides that the President is elected by electors chosen by each state, rather than by the direct vote of the people. For this reason, Presidents have been elected even though they lost the popular vote. It has been the case with five presidents. In 2000, Al Gore lost to Bush even though Gore had 50,000 more popular votes. In 2016, Trump was elected even though Hillary Clinton had 2.8 million more popular votes.

The Constitution provides that each state shall have two senators, but it provides that the number of congressional representatives shall be determined by a state's population. Accordingly, Wyoming has only one representative, whereas other states have many.

Money: It costs a lot to run a political campaign because of the cost of advertising and various activities. A good example of the role money plays is Sen. Kyrsten Sinema. According to an Associated Press article dated August 15, 2022, that appeared in Fortune:

"Sen. Kyrsten Sinema, the Arizona Democrat who single-handedly thwarted her party's long-term goal of raising taxes on wealthy investors, received nearly $1 million over the past year from private equity professionals, hedge fund managers, and venture capitalists whose taxes would have increased under the plan.

For years Democrats have promised to raise taxes on such investors who pay a significantly lower rate on their earnings than ordinary workers, but just as they closed in on that goal last week, Sinema forced a series of changes to her party's $740 billion election year spending package eliminating a proposed carried interest tax increase on private equity earnings while securing a $35 billion exemption that will spare much of the industry from a separate tax increase other corporations now have to pay."

The Supreme Court: The Supreme Court's role is explained well at the Citizens Take Action website:

"Believe it or not, before some recent Supreme Court decisions, the American political system was not always so skewed in favor of the wealthy and powerful. In fact, dating back to the Tillman Act of 1907 and the Taft-Hartley Act of 1947, Congress has limited the ability of corporations and labor unions to make contributions or expenditures in connection with political campaigns.

The influx of money from corporations, unions, and ultra-wealthy individuals in recent decades is due largely to a few poorly reasoned Supreme Court decisions."

The website singled out one case, Citizens United v. FEC:

"In a ruling that directly contradicted previous precedent set in *Austin,* the court held that **even though corporations are unique entities that receive special benefits, those special benefits do not justify prohibitions on corporate political speech**. In other words, after Citizens United, corporations and unions are free to spend unlimited amounts of money to influence elections. The court also went so far as to claim that censoring corporations has "muffled the voice that best represents the most significant segments of the economy" and that by limiting corporate political speech, the electorate has been deprived of information, knowledge, and opinion vital to its function."

Ultimately, the court overruled *Austin* because the Government may not suppress political speech on the basis of the speaker's corporate identity. No sufficient governmental interest justifies limits on the political speech of nonprofit or for-profit corporations.

Citizens United was followed by decisions that led to the creation of Super PACS, which are not bound by spending limits. According to the Brennan Center for Justice, "From 2010 to 2022, Super PACS spent approximately $6.4 billion on federal elections. In the 2024 election, they set a record of at least $2.7 billion."

A reading of the briefs submitted to the Supreme Court in Citizens United leads me to believe that the Justices knew, or should have known, that the decision would lead to a huge increase in contributions by high-net-worth individuals and businesses. Worse, the decision reinforces concerns that a majority of Supreme Court Justices are aligned with the interests of the wealthy and large corporations.

Concern About the Future

Not previously mentioned, but it is one of the biggest concerns about the future: Climate Change. Notwithstanding the denial by President Trump, the climate is changing, and the changes are and will be massive. A quick visit to the NOAA website spells out where and how the changes will occur. It is critical for people to evaluate their own situation, including where they live and where they work.

As the previous discussion has pointed out, major changes have taken place in many industries, and new technologies are rapidly emerging. Who knows today what artificial intelligence will produce in the future? So young people must seriously consider the career or careers they choose and how amenable they are to change. The Apollo technical website has these statistics:

"It is estimated that most people will have 12 jobs during their lives. In the last year, 32% of those aged 25 to 44 have considered a career change. Since starting their first job after college, 29% of people have completely changed fields.

One of the main factors for these changes is the desire for a salary increase (**39**%), or the interest in a **different field (21%),** and those looking for upward mobility came in at 20%.

The same survey found that many Americans who pursued a specific major do not use it at work. In fact, **21%** use all of their education, **53%** use half or less of their education, and **15% use none of their education** in their current job."

Although not easy, I believe young people should constantly seek opportunities to establish their own businesses or to join a business as a principal, not as an employee. They should look for situations where people with money are struggling and would be amenable to paying for assistance. They should also look at poorly run small businesses and see whether they can be acquired on good terms and made profitable.

As I came out of law school, I never expected to be in the broadcast or cable television business.

Young people should also be prepared for failure. I have had a couple of failures. Some years ago, when I was a member and, for a brief period, a director of the Paso Fino Horse Association, I thought it would be a great idea to form groups of Paso Fino pleasure riders, so I came up with the Paso Fino Cavalry. With others, I put together a newsletter and purchased some jackets with the Cavalry prominently displayed. I did not expect to make money with the Cavalry, but I did hope to increase the breed's popularity. The cavalry bombed. We did produce one great newsletter, but that was it.

My most recent failure concerns climate change. With the help of a couple of people, I came up with the trademark— **"Save Our Future"**, which has a color map of the northern hemisphere at 0. I purchased hundreds of T-shirts and caps that prominently feature the logo. It too had bombed.

My novels also failed from a marketing standpoint, and they did not sell mainly because I did not know how to promote them. But I am besieged with requests from a company that claims it can market them.

Apart from all the concerns mentioned, my biggest concern is that so many people are voting against their own interests, which, in my view, could be a fatal blow to our political and administrative system in the future.

This Book would not be complete without mentioning a few other things:

- I love dogs. Gail and I got our first dog when we were living in an apartment in Cambridge, Massachusetts, while I was in law school. It was a Scotch Terrier, Gail's favorite breed. We subsequently had more Scotties, including Sparky, who was a fantastic dog. I became interested in larger dogs, particularly German Shepherds. My first Shepherd was Black. He loved Gail and me, but had one huge problem – he was a biter. He would be standing with us as we talked to people, then suddenly bite them. He bit three or four people and finally bit one too many. Gail and I were going out of town and were putting him in a dog boarding place when he bit the woman who was taking him. I immediately took him to our vet, where she put him down. I hugged him as the shot took hold, and he seemed to understand what was happening and why. I was determined to get another German Shepherd, but it absolutely could not be a biter. I did considerable research and found two things.

- First, a kennel in Marengo, Illinois, that was highly rated for producing good family dogs. Second, I discovered a German Shepherd book that includes a temperament test for puppies at only 7 weeks old. It called for various movements to be made and a puppy's reaction. I went to the breeder with the test. It had a litter of newly born Shepherds. I said I wanted the litter tested and said I would buy the one thing that did the best. On test day, the breeder brought out a puppy and said it would be the winner. It failed the test. They brought out the other puppies and one aced the test. I bought him, and he was outstanding. Subsequently, I have bought more Shepherds from the breeder, and they all have had outstanding temperaments.

- As mentioned earlier, Gail got me interested in horses. I started out with quarter horses. My first horse was old but great. His name was Earl, and he was a pleasure to ride. I could take him on trail rides with the Lake County posse. One of our friends said I needed to have a horse with more energy, so we got Lucky. I took Lucky for a test ride, and he seemed to be great. We were living in Libertyville, Illinois. Near our place was a riding facility. One day, my daughter Susan and a friend of hers went on a trail ride with me. We had been gone for a while when Susan and her friend decided to return to the riding facility. They decided to gallop. I did not join them and restrained Lucky. He bucked me off, and I landed on the ground in pain. Susan and her friend came back and called the fire department, which sent an ambulance that took me to a hospital in nearby Waukegan. The doctors did an X-ray and said there were no broken bones. They sent me home. Subsequently, when Gail and I went to Scottsdale, I had a physical at the Mayo Clinic, where they told me I had broken five ribs. There was another episode where Lucky bucked me off, and we sold him, emphasizing that he needed to be with an experienced rider. We talked to the buyer about a year later.

He told us how great Lucky was, but then paused and said, "There's only one thing, one day when I was walking him, he suddenly bucked me off."

- I was fortunate to learn about Paso Fino horses. They are smaller than Quarter Horses and, most importantly, are gaited – the ride is smooth and not up and down as is the case with Quarter Horses. I fell in love with it, rode it, and showed it extensively. Some of my happiest days were trail riding Rain Dancer in the forests in Flagstaff. At one point, I became a member of the Paso Fino Association Board of Directors. A majority of the members were nasty, and I couldn't wait to get off the Board. Subsequently, when Gail and I were in Scottsdale, we showed and bred Arabian horses. We still have one. His name is Pogo. He was born in our place. When he was a yearling, we showed him at the Scottsdale Arabian horse show in an amateur one-year-old halter class. There were sixty horses in the class. Pogo came in First, and we won Ten Thousand Dollars. We kept showing Pogo both in halter and riding classes, but he did not excel. Finally, after seeing him standing in a stall at a trainer's facility, we decided to take him home. He is with us now and is the happiest horse in the World. He has a big stall with a big turnout and spends mornings in an arena with other horses,

- I love to travel and have traveled extensively. Gail and I were early travelers to China after the "opening up." We have traveled to several countries in Asia, Europe, and South America, many times on cruise or river ships. I also took a cruise to Antarctica, where I went ashore at various places. Two African safaris and a river trip in Vietnam were outstanding. I took many photographs during my travels and had many of them collected in books. During my trip to Antarctica, one of my photos was selected as the best, and I was given a great book about Ernest Shackleton's Antarctic Expedition, autographed by members of the ship's crew.

- Perhaps because I have had to keep busy, I wrote two novels – *TM and the Little White Dog* and *TM and the Missing Coed*. In both cases, I was assisted by a special Amazon unit that was very helpful in reviewing my writing and offering suggestions.

www.ingramcontent.com/pod-product-compliance
Lightning Source LLC
Chambersburg PA
CBHW050220270326
41914CB00003BA/490